TRUE OR FALSE?

1. People and companies that win in this fast-paced environment react quickly to change and new opportunities.

2. You can be successful by being slower than your competition.

3. Listening to your customers is the most important key to business success.

4. In a tight economy and hyper-competitive business environment, vacations need to be postponed.

5. Successful companies can ignore their competition.

Answers on next page

In this book, Robert Kriegel, bestselling author of
Sacred Cows Make the Best Burgers **and**
If It Ain't Broke…Break It! **helps you see yourself,**
your company, and your career in a whole new light.

Top Praise for Robert J. Kriegel

"A must-read! Fun and practical. Shows you how to lead people through a myriad of changes and challenges confronting all of us today."

—Ken Blanchard, coauthor of *The One-Minute Manager*® and
Everyone's a Coach, on *Sacred Cows Make the Best Burgers*

"Remarkable…matchless….I am inspired by it."

—Tom Peters, author of *In Search of Excellence*,
on *Sacred Cows Make the Best Burgers*

ANSWERS

*1. **False**. Winners in these times *create* change and new opportunities; get proactive, not reactive. (p. 6)

*2. **True**. Some of America's biggest, best companies have learned that the shortest route to breakthrough ideas is often the slowest one. (p. 68)

*3. **False**. One hundred years ago, farmers wanted a better horse and plow, not a tractor. It's not your job just to meet your customer's needs; you need to *anticipate* them. (p. 201)

*4. **False**. Successful companies realize their employees are more productive and creative if they can "unplug" from work. (p. 43)

*5. **True**. In the words of one of America's most successful businessmen: "We never look at our competitors' products. Why should we assume they know what they're doing?" (p. 127)

HOW TO SUCCEED
IN BUSINESS
WITHOUT WORKING
SO DAMN HARD

HOW TO SUCCEED IN BUSINESS WITHOUT WORKING SO DAMN HARD

ROBERT J. KRIEGEL

WARNER
BUSINESS
BOOKS ™

NEW YORK   BOSTON

Copyright © 2002 by Kriegel 2 Inc.

Warner Business Books

Warner Books
Time Warner Book Group
1271 Avenue of the Americas, New York, NY 10020
Visit our Web site at www.twbookmark.com.

The Warner Business Book logo is a trademark of Warner Books, Inc.

Printed in the United States of America
Originally published in hardcover by Warner Books, Inc.

First Trade Printing: September 2003
10 9 8 7 6 5 4 3 2

The Library of Congress has cataloged the hardcover edition as follows:

Kriegel, Robert J.
    How to succeed in business without working so damn hard : rethinking the rules, reinventing the game / Robert J. Kriegel.
    p. cm.
    Includes bibliographical references.
    ISBN 0-446-52632-0
    1. Success in business. 2. Time management. 3. Organizational change.
I. Title.

HF5386 .K854 2002
650.1—dc21   2001045588
        ISBN: 0-446-67986-0 (PBK.)

To Marilyn, my lover, coach, editor, pal, soul mate,
and life partner, for helping me to get out of my niches
and ruts, for inspiring me with your creativity and integrity,
and for your continuing support and encouragement.

Acknowledgments

Many, many, many thanks to:

Caryn Stanley, for managing my office, my schedule, and a lot
of my life, and for going beyond what I thought possible with
care, creativity, and a great sense of humor.

Lisa Ruggiero for the extra effort you gave on this project and
for adding warmth and fun to our office.

My son and best friend, Otis, for your love, support, creativity,
and the incredible ability to get me to laugh and not take myself so seriously.

Rob McMahon for your terrific editing and friendship.

Mark Rosenblatt for your innovative ideas and hands-on help.

Katina Matson and John Brockman, as always, for your profes-
sionalism in representing me as well as for the great times had
hanging out together.

Susan Suffes, Mike Stanley, and Myrtle Harris for your friendship, continued support, and creative feedback.

The friends at my speakers' bureaus for continually recommending me.

All who have participated in my programs and attended my speeches.

Contents

CHAPTER 1

Working Harder Works But . . .

You know you are working too damn hard when:

➠ You always feel like you're behind, running a little late.
➠ You are irritable, critical, or short-tempered.
➠ You see less and less of your friends and family.
➠ You get more headaches and stomachaches.
➠ You have a tough time relaxing.
➠ You feel guilty when you aren't working.
➠ It's all work and no play.
➠ You're married to your job.
➠ You tire easily.
➠ You have trouble falling asleep.
➠ You sometimes feel depressed or sad without any apparent reason.
➠ You need to be continually busy.
➠ You're not having much fun.

The secret of my success is simple. I just work harder than anyone else," said the first of four speakers on a superstar panel at a national convention of mortgage brokers. She then went on to describe her typical workday, which began at five A.M. and ended at about ten P.M. and consisted of calling on realtors, sending out weekly update sheets, writing new ads, attending open houses, shaking lots of hands, and endless schmoozing and boozing.

The next two speakers practically lip-synched her words.

I was exhausted just listening. A great success strategy, I thought—for not having a life.

MACHO WORK ETHIC

It's no secret that people are buying into this marathon madness as their strategy for success. These days the average workweek is sixty hours and rising. The average business lunch is thirty-six minutes and falling. And a ninety- to one-hundred-hour workweek is the norm for many young hounds on the scent of the big score.

My seatmate on a recent flight, a young man in his early thirties who worked for one of the big five accounting firms, told me that his normal workweek was one-hundred-plus hours. And he was bragging about it as if it were an indication of how "cool" he was.

I often overhear people boasting about the meeting the previous night that lasted until two A.M. For these folks, success is directly related to the number of hours they spend at the office. As if the longer and harder they work, the more they will be looked at as superheroes. What isn't admitted— or possibly even realized—is that when you work that late, your brain is too fried to be productive. Quality and creativity rarely emanate out of an exhausted mind. More mistakes are made when you're tired or pumped on caffeine, which means having to redo in the light of day what you did at night.

"The last company I worked at had five different design teams. And there was a crazy contest that occurred at the end of the day," Mike McDevitt, a Clio Award–winning graphic and Web site designer in New York City, told me. "No one wanted to be the first to leave. There was a stigma about it. It meant that you weren't doing your job or working hard enough. Or that you were a wuss. It's as if people's self-worth was directly related to how late they stayed at the office."

The Price

No matter how tough you think you are, the stress result-ing from this work-longer-and-harder strategy is enormous. And that stress doesn't magically disappear at the end of the workday. You don't just leave your office and instantly trans-form into a relaxed, easygoing person.

As a culture, we have become more irritable, quick-tempered, cranky, and negative. Witness the outbreak of road rage and airline rage. We consume over fifteen tons of aspirin and roll upon roll of Rolaids in an effort to combat the ner-vous minds and jumpy stomachs caused by stress. Depressing? Well, more than twenty-two million people are taking mood-lifting drugs like Prozac and Zoloft.

Quality time with your spouse? Romantic evenings? Great sex? *Fuhgeddaboudit!* Over 50 percent of marriages end in di-vorce. Seen your kids lately? Been to a Little League game or the play they were in? A study of one thousand third to twelfth graders by Ellen Galinsky, cofounder of the Families and Work Institute, revealed that what's most important to chil-dren is that their parents bring less stress home from work and focus more on them when the family is together.[1]

Yet the children of today's workforce, shuffled and shuttled from dance class to soccer practice to homework to bed, are managed rather than loved. And we wonder why so many have problems and act out.

Vacations, if taken at all, have become long weekends with a cell phone in the golf bag or a beeper in a backpack. It's no wonder that so many people are asking the same tough ques-tion: "How come, if I'm so successful, I'm not having more fun? And if I'm so 'together,' why do I feel so out of control?"

The high stress level obviously leads to burnout, so it's not surprising that a *Wall Street Journal*/ABC News poll found that more than half of all Americans would choose a new line of work if they had the chance.

Yeah, But!

"I'm going to work at this place for another couple of years, and then cash in and get out of the rat race," my hundred-hour-workweek seatmate told me. Many like him are willing to put up with the stress and sacrifices in their pursuit of the big payola.

The problem is not only that this "run, run, rush, rush, race, race" strategy creates stress and limits the quality of life, but, as you will see in forthcoming chapters, this work style also hinders performance, productivity, and creativity. "It's tempting to link the United States productivity boom to the long hours American workers put in, but it just ain't so," writes Ted Fishman, a business reporter for *USA Today*. "Mindy Fried, a researcher at the Center for Work and Family, has found that overworked employees suffer from more stress and become less productive and capable than more rested ones. U.S. companies that have cut workers' hours have seen worker morale and productivity improve. They also have more success retaining employees. By American standards, the Dutch, who work a mere 1,370 hours a year, compared to our 2,000 plus, might look slothful. Think again. Their economy is the most productive in the world."[2]

A Passionate 80 Percent

You may be thinking, "What is Kriegel telling me to do? Give up my dreams and go to work for the Motor Vehicle Bureau?" Not at all. What's needed is not a new line of work but a new way of thinking. I'm not suggesting that you *change* your game, but rather change the way you play it.

The type of thinking I am talking about occurred at the mortgage brokers' convention discussed at the beginning of the chapter. After hearing the first three superstars talk about their marathon strategies, I was ready to slip out of the session. But the first words of the last speaker, Scott Beaman, who was the top producer in the country, stopped me halfway up the aisle. "My strategy," he said, "is to give a passionate *80 percent* effort. I work my butt off six hours a day, five days a week."

Beaman outlined a totally different strategy then the previous three workaholics. His day wasn't made up of racing madly to open houses, sending out mailers, phoning prospects. His approach was to go to the local Chamber of Commerce to find out what companies were moving into the area. Then he would contact each company's human resource director and get a list of the people being transferred.

He would e-mail these people and schedule a meeting at their company headquarters prior to their move. His presentations would include videos, slides, and handouts with information on housing, schooling, and other concerns about the area. He would also prequalify them for mortgages, find out their specific needs, and, upon his return, send them any additional information they requested.

Rather than competing with the other mortgage brokers, Beaman had changed the game. His success was not a result of working harder and longer, but of bold and innovative thinking. Beaman had broken out of the old mortgage broker "box" by rethinking the rules of the game and redefining his role with the customer. Reinventing the game enabled him to become successful without having to work as hard or as long as his sweating, sleep-deprived competitors.

"I used to be a work-a-maniac like most people in my field," Beaman told me, "but I realized that though I was doing well, I didn't have a life. I was missing seeing my kids grow up, and my relationship with my wife was lousy.

"So I took a time-out, stepped back from the action, and analyzed my game. Rethinking my approach helped me to realize that there were lots of new companies moving into our area, which meant lots of people who were going to be looking for housing and mortgages. So rather than wait for them to come to me, I flipped the rules around and went to them. I'm much more successful now, and I spend more time with my kids. I go to all their games and recitals and my home life is great."

PIONEERING

Working hard does work. It's the American ethic. And it definitely can lead to success. But as you can see from the innovative strategy that Scott Beaman created, as well as the many others that will be discussed throughout this book, it's not the only way. The American ethic is also one of a pioneering spirit, of exploring new territory, and of taking the path less trod. It is one of creating change, rather than responding to market shifts and new opportunities, and of being out in front of the wave, rather than trying to keep up with it.

The world is changing at an incredible pace. Mergers, acquisitions, and consolidations are happening at the speed of light in every industry, creating big new competitors with deep pockets and long reaches. The economy is unpredictable. Customers are more demanding and less loyal. Technology that evolves every time we turn around has changed—and will continue to change—the way we communicate, obtain information, sell our goods, and run our businesses. It is also transforming how, where, when, and what we buy, as well as who we buy from. And this pace of change will only speed up, not slow down.

To succeed in these rapidly changing times, whether you are an entrepreneur like Beaman or climbing the corporate ladder, it is necessary to challenge the old modes, myths, and mind-sets, and rethink, redefine, and reinvent your business philosophy. The innovative strategies discussed in this book will enable you to develop dramatic new solutions to old problems, create exciting new opportunities, and succeed beyond what you ever thought possible, all without having to work so *damn* hard.

))))⇒ **KEEP IN MIND**

))⇒ Working harder does work but it's not the only way to achieve your goals and realize your dreams.

---

[1] "Career Search," *San Francisco Chronicle*, 19 December 1999, p. 2.

[2] *USA Today*, 28 June 2000, Money section, p. 2.

CHAPTER 2

Rushing Slows You Down

FULL-TILT BOOGIE

This may surprise you, but one of the major causes of working too damn hard and not achieving the requisite results is our obsession with speed. *Speed* to market. *Speed* to manufacture. Faster modems to *speed* up communications. *Speed* up to develop and deliver products. *Speed* up to grow your business. *Speed* up to go public. Whatever you are doing, know that someone, somewhere, is trying to do it faster.

The result of this focus on *speed* is that everyone has shifted into high gear, rushing, racing, and running. The workplace has been inflicted with hurry sickness. It's full-tilt boogie time. No slow dancing allowed. What's the problem? you're thinking. You want speed; you've got to speed up.

Wrong! Speed doesn't come from rushing. The opposite is true. Rushing actually slows you down.

Redoing What You've Done

When you are in a hurry, you make more mistakes. The Quality College says people make 20 to 25 percent more mistakes when in a hurry. The consequence of making these mistakes is that you have to do whatever you did over again. So in your rush, the mistakes you make cause you to take even more time to do your work.

The rule is that if you don't *take* the time to do it right the first time, you'll have to *make* the time to do it right the second time. An internal consultant at Nabisco recently told me that a company survey revealed that people in the company broke down their work as such: 15 percent doing value-added work, 20 percent doing necessary work, 20 percent doing unnecessary work, 15 percent not working at all, and, get this, *30 percent of their time doing rework.* The cause of the rework, according to this consultant, was people rushing around and quickly making decisions without thinking them through.

These mistakes aren't the "good" mistakes you make when experimenting with new ideas and thinking "out of the box." The mistakes I'm talking about are the careless ones caused by rushing. The ones that can be easily corrected the second time around. But these small mistakes, besides wasting time and energy, cause people to lose confidence and trust in you.

Overlooking the Basics

Sometimes these seemingly small mistakes can be extremely costly. Often employees, even whole departments, are in such a rush that they overlook some of the basics. An executive in the beer industry told me about a competitor that had developed an accelerated brewing process that significantly cut the time it took to brew the beer, as well as the cost. Everyone was excited because this innovation was going to provide a competitive edge.

The rush was on to get to market as quickly as possible. This involved developing new promotions, new advertising, new packaging, and new sales materials. They got to market in record time and the cost savings allowed them to sell the beer at a significantly lower price than the competition. And customers were buying it at a record pace. It was only then that they discovered that in their haste to get to market fast, they forgot one small, essential step. They forgot to taste the beer. Their next step was to recall all the products at a record pace, causing everyone to speed up even more.

Space Cadets

Then there is the mistake that resulted in the loss of a $125 million spacecraft as it approached Mars. The internal review team at NASA's Jet Propulsion Lab concluded the error was caused because Lockheed Martin, the builders of the spacecraft, specified certain measurements in pounds whereas NASA scientists thought the information was in the metric measurement of newtons.[1]

The miscalculation went undetected for months during the design, building, and launching phases, and caused the Mars Climate Orbiter to be off target by sixty miles. "The real issue is not that the data was wrong," said Edward Stone, the director of the Jet Propulsion Lab, who was in charge of the mission. "The real issue is our process."[2] A rocket scientist I spoke with assured me the real reason was the enormous pressure on these labs to get everything done yesterday.

Experts wondered why something so basic could have gone undetected for so long. "Last time I checked, I could visually sort out the difference between a foot and a meter,"[3] said John Pike, director of Space Policy at the Federation of American Scientists.

When people are in a hurry, they often take the basics for granted and forget to check and recheck. "Who's got time to recheck?" is the prevailing thinking. The worst nuclear power accident in Japan's history occurred as a result of a hurry-up environment. Workers accidentally poured 35 pounds of uranium into a purification tank instead of the 5.2 pounds normally used, causing an out-of-control chain reaction.[4] "How could that have happened?" I asked an engineer at General Electric who was a specialist in nuclear power. "People overworked and burned out, trying to get everything done in a hurry," was his response. The same thing happens in hospitals where overworked staffs desperately try to get more done in less time.

GROWING TOO FAST

Everyone is into warp-speed growth these days: bigger companies, more people, more revenues, more profit. And it's not just that they want to grow but that they want to grow faster than the next guy. The problem with growing too fast is that you often don't make good decisions. It's as if you try to stretch a muscle too far and too fast. You will strain the muscle, possibly tear it and do irreparable damage. Similarly in business. The rush to growth can cause self-inflicted wounds.

Procter & Gamble's $36 billion plunge in market value in early 2000 was caused, it is believed, by CEO Durk Jager trying to move faster and bring on more change than people could handle. "He's been moving too quickly," said Deutsche Bank analyst Andrew Shore. "Speed can't be the most important thing."[5]

Look what happened to Webvan, the online supermarket whose stock at the time of this writing is selling at thirty four cents, which is down *99 percent* from their high. The problem, according to analysts, is that they tried to expand to twenty-six cities with a complex and expensive automated distribution system before proving that the model could work. "They needed to operate in one market, get their model perfect, and show they could have a positive cash flow," said Lauren Levitan, an analyst at Robertson Stephens. "No one has ever gone public with a national roll-out with zero markets performing to plan."[6]

London Fog is another example. In surveys taken in the early nineties it had a 92 percent brand-name recognition and was probably the best-known manufacturer of raincoats in the country. Yet at the end of the decade, it filed for Chapter 11. Why? They tried to grow too fast. "First going beyond outerwear and into sportswear, then deciding to open up small stores, then to become a big-box retailer like Wal-Mart and Home Depot and go into strip centers. Since they are into weather gear, they said, 'Let's go into airports and train stations.' It all failed miserably,"[7] says retail consultant Mark Millman.

"If a company invests faster than it learns, it will over drive the opportunity and end up with an expensive and embarrassing failure," writes Gary Hamel. "That's the fate that befell Apple's pioneering handheld computer, the Newton. Was there a potential market out there for palm computers? Sure. Could investment and marketing hype alone force the market to develop on Apple's time frame. NO."[8]

Discussing excite@home's $7.28-billion loss and drop in stock price from $100 to less than 20 cents, John Corcoran, Internet analyst at CIBC World Markets, said the problem for this company, which had been the nation's leading provider of fast Internet service, was: ". . . trying too many things at once, at too high a velocity—they were growing for growth's sake, grow at all costs . . ."[9]

Grow Slow

"Don't let growth seduce you. When you're growing fast, the temptation is to keep increasing your growth rate," says Michael Bloomberg, one of Wall Street's most successful entrepreneurs and the founder and CEO of Bloomberg LP, whose terminals are used by more than 250,000 people in ninety-seven countries. "You get euphoric. You think you can walk on water. You think you're smarter than everyone else. This is exactly what gets companies into trouble. It's hard to say, 'Let's slow down.' But that's what you have to do."[10]

"The question is not 'To grow or not to grow?' but how fast

to grow. If you grow too fast, you recruit too fast and you're more likely to make mistakes down the road. Our strategy has been to grow very slowly,"[11] says Andy Law, the chairman of St. Luke's Communications Ltd., a London advertising agency. Law takes on a maximum of three pieces of new business a year. Last year St. Luke's turned down a $90 million client because they had already reached their limit. Law thinks if you grow too fast, you become less inventive. His slow-growth strategy seems to be working just fine. Last year his revenues increased by 75 percent.

All Mouth, No Ears

It is only after understanding your customer's needs, concerns, and goals that you will be able to come up with innovative ideas. Ultimately it boils down to making a connection with another human being. The same is true for selling internal customers or working with a team to develop new ideas. It's all about creating relationships.

We've all been allotted the right equipment in the right proportion in order to be great at relationships—two eyes, two ears, and one mouth. The problem is that when we're in a rush, the proportion becomes inverted. It's as if we have nine mouths and nothing else. When racing in fast-forward, we talk too much, talk too fast, talk too loud, and don't look, listen, or connect.

"In the last year, we overestimated how much change we could ask people to assimilate to and still focus on the customer,"[12] said Anthony J. Ricci, an executive vice president at Sears. Ricci went on to say that overloading employees resulted in decreased customer-satisfaction levels and decreased sales.

Faster Past

The rush-rush mind-set not only causes more mistakes and impedes communication, it also hinders creativity and innovation.

"What we lose, as just about everything accelerates, is the chance to reflect, to analyze," wrote noted author and scholar Barbara Ehrenreich in a *New York Times* review of James Gleick's book *Faster*. "Unfortunately, deep concentration . . . isn't as fast as an electron tunneling through silicon. Like composting, it takes time for the pattern of neural firing to shift and connect and for whole new patterns in our minds to develop" [which is what innovation and out-of-the-box thinking is all about]. "Try to shorten that time and you move very quickly from diverted to distracted, from clever to glib. Faster is fun," continues Ehrenreich, "but slower might have got us a whole lot further along."[13]

Harebrained

Monty Python alumnus John Cleese, in addition to being a great comedian and the "Minister of Funny Walks," has a law degree from Cambridge. Cleese, who also has a very successful management training business, recalls the analogy of the tortoise and the hare. "The problem in business is that there is no room for the tortoise mind, a terribly dangerous development that stifles creativity and innovation and inevitably leads to bad decisions," says Cleese. "The widely held belief is that being decisive means making decisions quickly, that fast is always better. Although making decisions fast looks impressive,"[14] Cleese cautions that it reduces your chances of coming up with the right answer as well as an innovative one.

Cleese advises that both the hare and the tortoise need each other. The hare, which is similar to the left brain, thinks linearly, logically, and quickly. The tortoise, or the right brain, is more dreamy, and creative. Each has a role. "Unfortunately, the pressures of all kinds—deadlines, peers—give license to the hare brain to bully the tortoise. People need to make boundaries in time and space, like closing their door or going for a walk, to let their tortoise mind do its meandering work,"[15] says Cleese.

Sit on Your Hands

An activity that demands clear thinking and speed is chess. But the danger in chess, even though the clock is running, is making decisions too quickly. "Most players see a good move and they make it. That's an error," says chess master Viktor "the Terrible" Korchnoi, one of the world's top players. "You should never play the first good move that comes into your head. Put that move on your list, and then ask yourself if there is an even better move. I have seen [world champion] Gary Kasparov practically sit on his hands to keep himself from making a good move. If you see a good idea, look for a better one—that's my motto,"[16] says Korchnoi.

Many of us would make better decisions and develop more innovative strategies by heeding this advice. Don't jump on the first idea just because it shows up. Check it out. Sit on your hands. Take a little time to look for a move that is better.

Innovation and Incubation

Imagine sprinting along a road, pumping your arms and legs as fast as you can, and then someone bounds by you with a pogo stick as if you were standing still. That's the difference between rushing and innovation. Rushing gets you moving faster. But real progress, the big leaps forward, come from innovation. Innovation, however, isn't possible when you are rushing. Innovation doesn't happen on demand. Innovation requires time for incubation.

"The faster we speed up, the less time we have to think, to

incubate, to ponder, to dream," says Joey Reiman, the founder of award-winning Brighthouse, a creative think tank with clients such as Delta Airlines and Coca-Cola. "Today, when marketing writers and art directors are given an assignment, they're also given less time. Their salaries are lucrative, their offices are spacious, but their ideas are getting smaller and smaller because the time they have to incubate is decreasing," writes Reiman. "It's clear that we can always find ways to do it faster. But if we are to think better, to be more creative, more original, we need more time to think. If you want to accelerate your thinking, you must slow down."[17]

➡ **KEEP IN MIND**
- ➡ Overtrying leads to underperforming.
- ➡ Rushing around kills quality, communication, and innovation.
- ➡ Hurrying up slows you down.
- ➡ Grow slowly.

[1] *New York Times*, 1 October 1999, p. A1.
[2] Ibid.
[3] Ibid.
[4] Ibid.
[5] *Fortune*, 2 April 2000, p. 40.
[6] *New York Times*, 19 February 2001, p. B1.
[7] *New York Times*, 3 October 1999, p. B7.
[8] *Fortune*, 3 September 2001, p. 192.
[9] *Sacramento Bee*, Associated Press, 4 October 2001, p. D1.
[10] *Fast Company*, August 1998, p. 74.
[11] Ibid, p. 81.
[12] *New York Times*, 15 January 1998, C3.
[13] *New York Times Book Review*, 12 September 1999, p. 9.
[14] *New York Times*, 7 February 1999, p. B14.
[15] Ibid.
[16] *Fast Company*, May 1999, p. 196.
[17] Joey Reiman, *Thinking for a Living*, (Marietta, Ga.: Longstreet, 1998) p. 30.

CHAPTER 3

Try Easier

SLOWING DOWN TO SPEED UP

I was always taught that you had to give 110 percent in order to excel. But while conducting time trials for Olympic track hopefuls, I had an experience that caused me to rethink the whole "try harder" approach. Noticing that the runners seemed overly tense and tight while trying to gain that last burst of speed, Bud Winter, the U.S. track coach, had them try running at 90 percent. The transition was amazing. Every runner had faster times practicing at 90 percent effort than they did at 100 percent or 110 percent. The old "give it everything you've got" approach didn't work as well as not giving it everything you've got.

After that experience, I began to notice that same thing in respect to other sports. Think about any sport you play. In golf, for instance, a long straight drive results from not swinging as hard. Or when you're playing far better than your norm in tennis or dancing down a ski slope with ease and grace, doesn't it always feel as if you weren't even trying?

Don't Go All Out

The pros know this. Tom Telles, the coach of Olympic great Carl Lewis, had Lewis run at 90 percent. Ray Evernham, former NASCAR crew chief of the year for Winston Cup winner Jeff Gordon, once said, "Sometimes I'll tell him [Jeff] to go out and bust me a lap and he'll drive the car hard, really work it, mash the pedal, drive down into a corner, jam the brakes, and mash the pedal again. Then I'll say, 'Now take it easy and drive a smooth lap,' and he actually improves his time."[1]

Bruce Lee, the martial-arts master, once said, "The less effort, the faster and more powerful you will be."

Don't Punch the Accelerator

John Smith, the former world record holder in the 440-meter race, has become one of the track world's foremost speed coaches. The many Olympic-medal-winning athletes in his stable include reigning 100-meter world champion and record holder Maurice Greene, alone with Jon Drummond, Ato Bolton, Inger Miller, and Marie-Jose Perec.

Smiths says, "Sprinters want to punch that accelerator. But if you hit it too soon, you'll run out of gas. People think that all a sprinter needs to do is to run all out, but that's so Hollywood. I want my sprinters to do just the opposite." There's a world of difference between haste and speed, Smith tells us. Haste doesn't win races. Taking your time just might. The guys who are tense, the guys who are straining, have lost the race. The race goes to the athlete who's in control. Guys who have run incredibly fast always say the same thing: "That was so easy."[2]

Smith's advice is just as appropriate for those trying to be first on the fast track at work. Punching the accelerator too hard will cause you to run out of gas before the finish.

Taking the Grunt Out

The career of former Brooklyn Dodger pitching great Sandy Koufax hardly started out as a stepping-stone to the Hall of Fame. After six years in the majors, his record was a paltry 36 wins and 40 losses. His problem was that even though he had a blinding fastball, he couldn't control it.

The turning point in his career came when he was scheduled to pitch the first half of a spring training game. When the pitcher who was scheduled for the second half missed his plane, Koufax volunteered to pitch the whole game. To ensure that Koufax did not wear himself out, Norm Sherry, his pitching coach, advised him to ease up slightly on his fastball. The rest, as they say, is history. Koufax learned from this experience that a fastball will behave better, and with just as much life and more control, if you throttle back a little. He pitched a no-hitter that game and said, "I came home a different pitcher from the one who had left."[3]

These days, when Koufax coaches young pitchers, he shares the lesson that took him six years to learn and ultimately saved his career: "Take the grunt out,"[4] he tells them.

AND AT WORK

Koufax's wisdom works in any area of your life, from pitching a ball game to pitching a new client. Taking the grunt out, just a little, will allow you to be more relaxed, think more clearly, be more in control, and perform at a peak level no matter what you are doing.

Think about a time when you were performing your best at work. It could have been when you were giving a presentation and had the group in the palm of your hand, or handling a tough negotiation or a customer service problem with style and ease, or zipping through that pile of paperwork on your desk. Isn't it true that when you are at the top of your game, whatever your game is, it always feels effortless, like 90 percent effort?

Feeling Ahead

"It feels really great to be ahead of schedule rather than always feeling behind, which is usually the case," Mike Stanley, a builder of custom homes, told me after a seminar we had attended ended an hour earlier than expected. "When I feel behind, I get scattered, rushing to try and catch up. When I am ahead, I move slower, I'm more relaxed, I think more clearly, come up with better ideas, and communicate more effectively with my crews. But here's the kicker: I get more done and with better quality at these times than when I am rushing around." We then explored ways of acting as if he were ahead of schedule and slowing down, even when he was behind.

Selling Easy

The strategy with many sales groups is for the salespeople to make as many calls as possible, the thinking being that more calls will result in more sales. Sort of like the ballplayer who thinks the more times he's at bat, the more hits he's going to get.

I have done experiments with over 150 sales groups, ranging from those making high-level executive calls to telemarketers. My approach is to have half the group make as many calls as they can. The other half is instructed to make fewer calls, to work at 90 percent effort.

In every instance the group that made less calls had at least 20 percent better results. Why? The phrase that always comes up is the "quality of the call." "I don't feel as rushed, so I can communicate better" is a typical response. The people who make less calls talk about feeling more relaxed and being able to listen better, to think more clearly and creatively, and to help be a better problem solver for their client.

Work Less

"I know that in the final analysis, workaholics are not business successes," says Patti Manuel, the president and chief operating officer of Sprint's long-distance division. "There are people at Sprint who work from sunup to well past sundown. They might make middle management, but then they get stuck. They can't lift their heads above the trenches, and . . . make horrible managers. I try to guard against that syndrome.

"I try to create an environment in which people get ahead because of their contribution, not because of the number of hours they log," continues Manuel. "I let people know that balance is important. I take off Wednesday afternoons to volunteer at my son's school. People who work too much have a massive amount of discipline, but they're not applying it in the right way."[5]

Banning the Midnight Oil

Silicon Valley start-ups are usually seen as lots of young people working marathon hours in the quest for stock options. Yet Ipswitch, Inc., whose software is widely used by computer programmers, actually discourages employees from burning the midnight oil. Roger Greene, the founder and president, talks to his employees about the need to take more personal days and vacation time. In fact, he recently increased the minimum employee vacation time to five weeks.

"A lot of people work really hard for thirty or forty years and then they retire and try to do all the fun things they didn't do before," Greene says. "I'd much rather live life as it comes along and do neat things while you're working and enjoy every year of your life."[6]

According to Art Beals, Ipswitch's CFO, "We downgrade the idea of being a workaholic. If somebody comes in on the weekends, they don't get praised for it. If people are doing extra work at night, you don't get admiration for that."[7]

With that philosophy, is it any wonder that Ipswitch's employee turnover rate is about 9 percent, roughly half the high-tech average? And revenues are up 33 percent this year to $22 million, with a profit of $4.3 million. Not bad for taking it a little easier, eh?

James Barksdale, the former CEO of Netscape, says that he tried to introduce some normalcy when he was at the company. "People were working twenty-hour days to make sure that Microsoft wouldn't run us out of business, so I started a

Netscape Escape Day once a month. People who work that hard burn out or get depressed and make mistakes. It comes back to haunt you."[8]

Pacing

Trying to work at 110 percent will cause you to burn out or blow out. Jeffrey Miller, a former vice president at Intel and now president and CEO of Documentum, a fast-growing software company, advises his people that "in order to prevent insanity, frustration, and burnout, they need to find their own pace. I learned this from my mentors at Intel," says Miller. "Each year, as I continued up the organization, I noticed I was working one hour longer. I also noticed that my mentor worked fewer hours than I did. I asked him what his secret was. He suggested figuring out a pace that I could keep up over the long term. I might have to sprint occasionally, but if I found the right overall pace, I'd be golden."[9]

Stewart Brand, whose thirty-year history of pioneering achievement includes launching the legendary *Whole Earth Catalog*, creating the New Games Tournament, and cofounding the Global Business Network, advises us that "if you want to keep speeding up, you'll also have to learn how to slow down."[10]

Don't Kick Back

I'm not saying that if you simply kick back and do nothing, you'll get great results. Those 90-percent-effort sales groups still made a lot of calls, and Carl Lewis and Maurice Green don't exactly loaf during a race. But to excel, you need to take the harried edge out of your efforts.

Trying Easier

Learning to "try easier" will improve not only your performance and creativity, but your quality of life. To remind me of this message, which is so counter to most of what I have learned in the past, I have a sign on my desk that says "90%" and a vanity license plate on my car that reads TRY EZR.

So whether you're trying to drop a few strokes in your golf game or add to your numbers at work:

))➤ **KEEP IN MIND**

➤ Take the "grunt" out and throttle back.

➤ Stretch, don't strain.

➤ When everything speeds up . . . slow down.

➤ Try easier: A passionate 90 percent effort is more effective, more productive, and more creative than a panicked 110 percent.

[1] *Fast Company*, October 1998, p. 178.

[2] *Fast Company*, May 2000, p. 181.

[3] *Sports Illustrated*, 12 July 1999, p. 98.

[4] Ibid.

[5] *Fast Company*, February/March 1999, p. 88.

[6] *Wall Street Journal*, 24 August 2000, p. B1.

[7] Ibid.

[8] *Forbes*, 4 September 2000, p. 36.

[9] *Fast Company*, August 1998, p. 80.

[10] *Fast Company*, May 2000, p. 394.

CHAPTER 4

Joe DiMaggio Never Bunted

DOING WHAT COMES UNNATURALLY

Nothing makes you work so damn hard as trying to do things that don't come naturally. Thomas K., the chief engineer for a telecommunications company, had recently been promoted to head of the division. The new position required keeping a staff of over 150 people motivated and performing at high levels, giving major presentations to top management and clients, and overseeing staffing and recruiting for the firm. Then there were the usual management responsibilities: forecasting, budgeting, keeping costs in line, and the mountains of paperwork.

Though Tom was great at solving intricate problems and developing innovative new designs, he was basically an introvert who was uncomfortable with people and terrified of giving large presentations. He also had little patience for all of the paperwork his new job required.

Wanting to succeed and move up the corporate ladder and increase his income, he set out to improve these skills. He took presentation workshops, hired a speaking coach, and even enrolled in a basic accounting course at a local university. Though he made improvements, he never became comfortable with all the interpersonal duties and continued to view the paperwork as his nemesis.

The bottom line was that Tom went from a job he loved and excelled at to one he hated and would never be better than mediocre at. After a year of trying to adapt, he took a leave of absence and eventually took a job as the chief design engineer with a competitor.

Promoting an individual isn't always advantageous to both parties. A promotion can result in highlighting a person's weaknesses. A top salesperson gets promoted to sales manager, a position requiring totally different skills, temperament, and duties, and not only doesn't like the new job but performs poorly. Similarly, many entrepreneurs fail miserably when they try to manage what they have started. Managing a business requires a whole different attitude and set of skills than starting one does.

Bruce Hubby, the chairman of Professional Dynametric Programs, whose surveys for evaluating people have been used by more than five thousand companies and three million people, says, "When people feel the need to act unnaturally, they experience the stress which lowers productivity and leads to job dissatisfaction. People are at their most productive when they're in a position that lets them draw on their natural strengths."[1]

Don't Shore Up Weak Spots

More often than not, the most you'll achieve when trying to improve in an area that is not a basic strength is mediocrity. And that ain't going to cut it in today's ultracompetitive market.

It's a struggle to improve at something you aren't naturally good at, and it also takes a lot of time and energy to make progress. And this is time that could be taken to enhance and maximize strengths that are keys to peak performance. In other words, the time taken to become mediocre is time that could be spent to become great at what you are already good at.

Joe DiMaggio probably could have learned to bunt, but that wasn't his strength or what he was paid to do.

Different Ladders

"Yeah, but if I want to make more money and have more say, I have to move up to management" is a typical response. OK, let's say you do move up to management and, as with Tom, it isn't your thing. Now, you're in a position that you not only don't like but have to work twice as hard in to achieve a level of competency. The truth is, you'll probably never be very good at the job. And if you're not good at it, you aren't going to be there for long.

Today many companies are recognizing this phenomenon and have created a new type of corporate ladder so that they are able to keep people in positions in which they can excel.

Eric B. was one of the top salesmen for a major life insurance company. But rather than promote him to management—which the company knew he wasn't cut out for—they created a senior position in which he could still call on clients.

But the new job, for which he received a substantial bump in salary, benefits, and perks, also consisted of training new salespeople, giving speeches at sales meetings, helping motivate the sales force, and working with those employees who were in a slump. Those were jobs that Eric excelled at, enjoyed, and was already doing in an unofficial capacity anyway.

This move benefited the company because Eric was out in the field and still producing. But they also gave him the opportunity to use his expertise to help train, develop, and motivate the sales force. So Eric not only increased his income, but he continued doing what he loved and did best. This was a win-win for everybody involved.

Build on Your Strengths

"Don't focus on building your weaknesses. Understand your strengths and place yourself in a position where these strengths count," advises management guru Peter Drucker. "Your strengths are what will carry you through to success."[2]

A monthly column featured in the *San Francisco Chronicle* posed the following question: "What should workers focus on more: building the strengths they already have or overcoming weaknesses?"

Marty Nemko, a career coach, syndicated columnist, and author of *Cool Careers for Dummies*, responded, "Study after study has shown that it's more fruitful to build on your strengths. Imagine a pair of identical twins with identical genes living in an identical environment. Each twin is terrific in math and lousy in writing. Now imagine that one worked at improving his math skills, while the other worked at improving his writing. Which twin would progress more? Which one will enjoy the learning process? Which one will become more marketable? Right. Work on building your strengths."[3]

Ellen Dilsaver, a senior vice president at Charles Schwab, advises, "Unless you have a fatal flaw, work on strengths and find roles that play to those strengths. Playing to your strengths such as communication skills or being able to network well or bring in new business not only energizes you but propels your career, because you are able to produce results and improve your skills so that you are superb."[4]

Working on your strengths is also more enjoyable, which makes it easier to improve and excel. The rapid success you achieve by maximizing your strong points further improves confidence and motivation, which then leads to more success. A positive, vital cycle is created.

Don't Improve Weaknesses

The same philosophy works when coaching. Based on interviews with over eighty thousand managers, Marcus Buckingham and Curt Coffman, analysts with the Gallup Organization and authors of the best-selling book *First, Break All the Rules*, found that great managers "focus on each person's strengths and manage around their weaknesses.

Don't try and fix the weakness. Don't try to perfect each person. Instead do everything you can to help each person cultivate their talents. Help each person become more of who they already are."[5]

"You don't need to know about people's weaknesses," adds Bruce Hubby. "You need to know about their strengths. Trying to correct a person's weaknesses can be a demotivator. People gain confidence when you build on their strengths."[6]

We are all different. Each of us has different talents, skills, aspirations, goals, and dreams. The role of a leader is to know the strengths of every member of the team and see that they each work at something that enables them to turn their passions and natural talents into expertise and peak performance.

FOCUSING ON CORE COMPETENCIES

Businesses of all kinds are being redefined and reinvented with this strategy in mind. They are topping off those areas that are not their strengths and focusing on core competencies. AT&T, Sprint, and MCI/WorldCom don't manufacture their phones or cables. Instead they focus on their strengths, which are their relationships to the customer and developing new ways to provide better service. Similarly, banks now concentrate on their relationship to the customer and outsource most of their backroom operations, including major parts of their credit and debit card operations, to companies who specialize in those areas.

Unlike many of its competitors, Cisco Systems, one of the most successful companies in the high-tech field, doesn't do any research for new product development. Recognizing that its strength is marketing and sales, it concentrates on acquiring companies and their products rather than spending time and money on research and development. "Instead of developing a new product line, Cisco acquires it, buying a young business and bringing it under their umbrella."[7] The company also outsources just about everything from manufacturing and assembling its routers to tracking inventory and shipping products. "It is getting to the point where products that Cisco sells may never be seen or touched by an actual Cisco employee," writes business columnist David Pescovitz.[8]

A major pipeline manufacturer was losing business because the cost of shipping the product to the work site, via their own trucking fleet, was significantly higher than the competition's cost. But try as they might, they couldn't reduce their expenses.

"Is trucking your area of expertise?" I asked.

"No," they replied, "it's designing, manufacturing, and installing pipeline at major highways and municipalities."

"So why not sell your trucks, outsource the shipping, and focus on your core competency, which is marketing and manufacturing the pipe?"

Hiring a trucking company to ship their pipe to the job site reduced their cost of shipping by 35 percent.

Use this lesson from corporate America—maximize your own effectiveness. Outsource anything that is not your personal core competency. Focus on your strengths and find partners or teammates who balance your own skills. If you're good at developing innovative new ideas but not so good at implementing them, find someone who is and team up with them. If you're a good starter, find a good finisher.

Strength Assessment

Take a minute and write down three of your strong points. Not things like "I am a good salesperson," "a good builder," or "a good coach." That is what you do, not who you are. Your strengths are personality traits, such as "creative," "empathetic," "outgoing," "analytical" . . . qualities that can be expressed in almost any type of situation, work or play.

To help individuals in my seminars gain a clear picture of their strengths, I have them answer the following questions:

1. Circle three of the following terms that most describe you, and combine them. Extrovert, Introvert, Creative, Analytical, Intuitive, Energetic, Staid, Positive, Cynical, Actor, Thinker, Starter, Finisher, Restless, Comfortable, Excitable, Calm, Risk Taker, Cautious, Great with People, Great Problem Solver, Loquacious, Quiet.

2. Review some of your past accomplishments. What were the main qualities that enabled you to achieve them?

3. Since loving to do something is usually a sign of a core competency, what are some of your hobbies or things you gravitate to in your spare time? What personal qualities do these activities give you an opportunity to express? For instance, mountain climbing might indicate a love of adventure, challenge, and risk taking. Doing crossword and jigsaw puzzles demonstrates a love of problem solving and working out details.

Leading from Strength

Utilizing your strengths enables you to be more productive, to perform better, and to thoroughly enjoy work. And when you have more fun, you are more creative, more motivated, and more effective.

The following exercises will help you excel and enjoy without having to work so damn hard.

Think of your current work:

- Are you utilizing your strengths on your job? Where and when?
- Where are some opportunities for you to further utilize your strong points?

- How could you redesign your job so that you make greater use of your core competencies?
- Design the perfect work for you, making the most of your strengths. Write the job description.
- Write a quarter-page ad for yourself.

➤ **KEEP IN MIND**

➤ Improving weaknesses is harder, less productive, less enjoyable, and takes more time than improving strengths.

➤ Don't try to be good at lots of things; instead, be great at one.

➤ Joe DiMaggio never bunted.

[1] *Fast Company*, November 1998, p. 88.
[2] *Boardroom Reports*, 1 July 1998, p. 13.
[3] *San Francisco Chronicle*, 3 December 2000, p. J1.
[4] Ibid.
[5] Marcus Buckingham and Curt Coffman, *First, Break All the Rules* (New York: Simon and Schuster, 1999), p. 137.
[6] *Fast Company*, November 1998, p. 88.
[7] *New York Times*, 27 September 2000, p. B6.
[8] *New York Times Magazine*, 11 JUNE 2000, p. 94.

CHAPTER 5

Time-Outs

An executive for a major fast-food chain was showing his schedule to the new CEO. "I want you to know I am always available," he told her. She looked at his overly full schedule with a genuinely puzzled expression, and asked very perceptively, "When do you get time to *think*?"

A recent study by the Pitney Bowes corporation found that the average corporate employee handled over fifty phone calls, twenty-plus e-mails, four pages, and three cell phone calls a day.[1] And that doesn't include faxes, voice mail, and snail mail. Based on my experience, these numbers are probably low.

If, for instance, you work ten hours a day, fifty phone calls alone means you are receiving five calls an hour. If they average just three minutes a call, you have just spent almost a third of your time at work on the phone. Not to mention reading and responding to faxes, e-mail, pagers, and going to lots of meetings.

The ethos today is "Never be out of touch." We carry our cell phones strapped to our belts the way cowboys carried their six-shooters. And feel just as naked without them. We go out for a round of golf with our cell phone in the golf bag. We hit the beach for some sun and surf but not without our pager resting in the shade of the beach bag.

BRAIN SHIFT

In my programs, I always ask, "How many of you get your best ideas—the barn burners, lightbulbs, the aha's—while at work?" No one ever raises their hand. "Which room in your house do you get your best ideas in?" I ask. The response is always the bathroom or bedroom. "Why is that?" "Because no one bothers me and I get time to think" is the usual response.

Yousuke Yamada, a lead engineer for Ricoh, the office equipment and camera maker, gets his best ideas while commuting to work on the train. "I cannot create an idea at my desk," he says. "I like to walk around a crowded train where nobody disturbs me."[2]

When I was teaching, several graduate school students did a study on where people get their best ideas. They found what you'd expect. It was while driving, exercising, taking a shower, taking a nap, or gardening. In other words, when people were not at work.

The best ideas emerge when people operate out of a different hemisphere of their brain. Normally, at work we do left-brain thinking, which is linear, rational, and logical. But the more innovative ideas come from the right brain, which is more creative and intuitive.

Creative Breaks

When I was working for Young & Rubicam Advertising, I decided to do a little research on creativity. I asked twenty of the top copywriters and art directors where and how they got their best ideas. None of them really knew where the ideas came from, but they all knew that they rarely came when they were at the office. And never, they told me, in meetings. They all agreed that good ideas always seem to come when you least expect them.

My own experience bears that out. People often ask me where I got the creative titles of my past books, *If It Ain't*

Broke . . . BREAK IT! and *Sacred Cows Make the Best Burgers.* The truth is that both of them came when I was in bed just musing and staring at the ceiling.

For seven years, I was a commentator for National Public Radio's *Marketplace* program. Every other week, I had to develop an innovative, entertaining commentary. But when I would sit at my computer trying to think of something to write, the blank screen always seemed like a reflection of what was on my mind. Nothing.

But without fail, the minute I would jump on my bike to go for a ride, ideas would start pouring out. For that reason I have learned never to leave home without my mini-tape-recorder.

Thinking Time

Does this mean that you should have a bed or a shower in your office? No, but what you definitely should do is take *thinking time.* People in some of the most high-pressure occupations, like sports, for instance, take a time-out. Why? To regroup, reenergize, rethink, restrategize.

Stepping back from the action provides you with a different perspective, allowing you to see a bigger picture.

In a recent speech, Ron Heifetz, author of *Leadership Without Easy Answers* and director of the Leadership Education Project at Harvard's Kennedy School of Government, pointed out that a leader needed to think about his organization from two points of view. Using a theater analogy, Heifetz said the leader must be both in the orchestra, close to the action, as well as in the balcony, far from it. The view from the balcony provides you with the big picture, which is critical for strategic thinking.

A major business magazine did a study of leaders from all fields and found that over two-thirds of them talked about spending a half an hour a day just thinking. Some would leave the building and take a walk, others would exercise, some talked about sitting and dreaming. All admitted that this was the time when they did their best thinking and got their best ideas.

Discussing the importance of this type of creative break, Tom Peters noted that Horst Schulze, the president of the Ritz-Carlton hotel chain, spends a half an hour every morning meditating on better ways to provide great customer service.[3] And he's the head of an institution renowned for fabulous customer service.

"You can always find reasons to work," says Carisa Bianchi, the president and CEO of innovative ad agency TBWA/Chiat/Day in San Francisco. "There will always be one more thing to do. But when people don't take time out, they stop being productive and creative. They stop being happy, and that affects the morale of everyone around them."[4]

Dr. Donald Hensrud, the director of the Mayo Clinic Executive Health Program, advises: "Try shutting your office door and closing your eyes for fifteen minutes. Lean back and breathe deeply. You'll be surprised at how this changes your perspective. Exercise, another winner, gives your mind a brief vacation while sending a surge of endorphins through your body. The time it takes to exercise can make up for itself in increased energy and efficiency, not to mention improved health down the road."[5]

The great Irish author George Bernard Shaw claimed that few people actually think more than two or three times a year. "I've made an international reputation for myself," he went on, "by thinking once or twice a week."

Back Burnering

People blanch at the thought of taking a time-out at work. They say, "I'm working as hard as I can just to keep up. Who's got the time?" My response is, you don't *not* have the time. Especially if you want to keep out in front of all the changes that are coming at you in this laser-fast environment.

It's important to understand that taking a short time-out to refuel and refresh doesn't mean that you are goofing off. When you take a break, your brain doesn't shut off. The ideas that you have been considering shift to a "back burner" where they incubate. The problems you've been working on make an unconscious shift from the left (logical) brain to the right (creative) brain. And then, boom! When you least expect it, the lightning strikes.

One of the ways to fuel the fires and activate your creative right brain is first to immerse yourself in the problem you are trying to solve. Learn everything you can.

Then stop thinking about it. Forget it! Focus on something else. I can almost guarantee that at some point the lightbulb will go off and you will get an important new insight.

A well-known syndicated columnist told me that when he gets stuck writing, he will stop and shift his attention. "I may do a menial task, some trashy reading, or even go to a movie. It's too bad there are no showers at work," he joked. "I don't have any hard-and-fast rules about what I should do at these times," he continued. "I know I have to take my mind off the article I am writing. My mind needs a rest. Invariably, either during or right after my break, I will get a flash—I don't know how else to describe it—that gives me some insight or perspective."

The president of a regional bank told me that when she got home from work and her mind was darting from one problem to another, she would change clothes and then go out and tinker with her car. "Sometimes I change the oil, clean a spark plug—do something for about twenty minutes. I have no idea whether I am doing the car any good," she told me. "But I am doing myself a world of good. It helps me to unwind. And I often get my best ideas when I'm working on the car."

Daydreaming

To stir the creative juices, Joey Reiman talks about the importance of taking creative breaks, which he calls daydreaming. "Daydreaming is at the heart of Brighthouse. Our belief is that the act of daydreaming, or what we prefer to call incubation, creates unheard-of and unthought-of possibilities. . . . It's important to be idle. People who keep busy all the time are generally not very creative."[6]

Paul MacCready's many innovations, which include the first successful solar-powered aircraft, have persuaded the American Society of Mechanical Engineers to name him the Engineer of the Century. At age seventy-five, he is still coming up with more new ideas than his creative team at Aero-Vironment can keep up with. According to MacCready, his best ideas occur away from work, "particularly when getting away on vacation, where you can relax, daydream, and let your mind wander." In fact, MacCready considers daydreaming his most productive activity.[7]

While walking in the halls with the CEO of a major high-tech company, the senior partner of a consulting company spotted a man sitting with his feet up on his desk and looking out the window. "What the heck is that guy doing?" he asked. "Exactly what we are paying him for—thinking," the CEO replied.

THE RED ZONE WILL BURN YOU OUT

Every engine runs on energy generated by either gas, electric, solar, or nuclear power. The human engine also runs on energy. The more you have at your disposal, the better you'll feel and perform and, as a result, the more productive and creative you'll be.

You can't keep running a high-performance engine in the red zone or it will burn out. Physical trainers also advise us that to get maximum efficiency from a muscle, it needs a recovery cycle. You can work one set of muscles one day, but you have to rest them the next day.

The same is true for your mental muscle. Without a rest, your brain will become fatigued and won't work as efficiently or effectively. When you are tired, you think less clearly and creatively and have less energy. You'll also make more mistakes. "I'm dead against workaholics. Working like that causes you to lose enthusiasm and vitality and inhibits creativity,"[8] Dick Munroe, the former chairman of Time Inc., told me.

An essential part of any conditioning program, whether mental or physical, is a recovery cycle, which means programming in some downtime. "Downtime" is really a misnomer. Taking a mini-break is actually an invaluable aid for increasing the quality of your "up time." Just a small break will help to refresh and reenergize you as well as provide new insights and perspectives.

Jim Loehr, a sports psychologist now working with businesspeople, and the author of *Mental Toughness*, writes, "To create optimal performance you have to address the management of energy at every level. . . . What we've found is very simple. The more ways that people are encouraged to oscillate—to move between stress—anything that prompts the expenditure of energy—and recovery—the happier they are, the better they perform, and the higher their productivity level."[9]

In the peak performance workshops I used to conduct, we gave participants three fifteen-minute "time-out" cards and told people that they had to use them each day.

Naps, Earphones, and Tai Chi

David Lunsford, the director of advanced technology for Dell Computer, says, "I often hear people proudly claim that they work one-hundred-hour weeks. The first thing I think is, how can a person really be effective for one hundred hours? How effective you are is more important than how long you work."[10] Lunsford, whose old work style resulted in two major burnouts, says he now schedules routine breaks in his workday to have private moments. One of the ways he does that is by just "sitting and reflecting for twenty minutes."[11]

There's no one best way to take a time-out. Everybody has a different style. What they all have in common is a break in routine. Jeffrey Sklar, a partner in Gruntal & Co., a New York City–based brokerage firm, has built a fifteen-minute deep-breathing break into the middle of his morning, and he takes that break no matter what else is going on. At lunch he takes at least a fifteen-minute walk, and at midafternoon he repeats his deep-breathing ritual. "Building more rest into my life was psychologically difficult, but I absolutely feel like I'm in a better zone now. My business is up 75 percent year to year, and a lot of that is managing my energy better."[12]

Harvey K., a broadcasting executive, says, "I've been a golf nut for years, so when my mind starts to race in all directions, I take out my putter and a few balls and practice putting for a couple of minutes on my office rug. It takes all of my attention to get the ball into the cup. This little break relaxes me, and I'm better able to focus when I get back to my work."

When he feels tired in the middle of the day or between patients, Dr. David Brandt, a psychologist and author, will put on earphones and listen to music. "The music relaxes me and gives me a lift, so that after five minutes or so I feel refreshed, energized, and ready to go again. The earphones are great because they drown out everything else."

"Rather than speed up when I am overwhelmed with phone calls from angry clients, copy changes, and shortened deadlines, I stop and do a five-minute routine I learned while studying tai chi," graphic designer Peter Bailey told me. "After finishing it, I feel like a new person—calmer, clearer, and with a lot more energy. These little breaks often give me a new perspective on what I was doing."

My wife, Marilyn, a psychologist and author, takes a five- or ten-minute nap when she feels her energy draining, and finds it never fails to energize her and get her ready for the next challenge. The amazing thing to me is that she often gets up from these little naps with an innovative new thought about what she was working on.

John Ancelet, the president of Vision Tech, an information recruiting company, takes fifteen-minute naps at work every day. And he thinks you should too. "I'm sure that a ten- to fifteen-minute nap will make you more productive during the day," says Ancelet.[13] Don't forget Thomas Edison and Winston Churchill were big on naps. And they were hardly unproductive.

I have found that doing moderate exercise, something that gets you breathing a little more heavily but not sweating, will give you a burst of energy. So when I feel sluggish at work, I often will do some push-ups and stomach crunches.

Vacations

Many people tell me they never take vacations because they're too busy. This is exactly the reason you should take one. "I have twenty weeks of vacation owed me," one engineer told me. And this response is more common than you might think. The type of schedule people are on these days is guaranteed to burn them out and result in a loss of energy, enthusiasm, productivity, and creativity.

Vacations are critical for mental, physical, and spiritual revitalization. I'm not talking about a golf vacation in which your cell phone gets more use than your putter. Nor am I suggesting that you go to the beach but call the office after every margarita. I'm talking about really getting away and not keeping in touch. Take a tip from the Dalai Lama, who advises us to once a year go to someplace we've never been before. The idea is to get as far away mentally as you can from your work.

Hewlett Packard, the world's second-largest computer company, operates more than most companies on voice mail. "But when I'm on vacation, skiing, or golfing," says Ann Livermore, the head of HP's Enterprise Computing Solutions

Organization, "I unplug. I don't even listen to my voice mail."[14]

"When I go on vacation, I don't even think about business," says Tony Morgan, a former governor of the BBC, chairman of several major corporations, and an Olympic silver medalist. "Then, when it's over, I'm excited about getting back to work. I'm enthusiastic and energized; my perceptions are sharper. I see things much more clearly than when I left."

"Every October, I spend some time on Cape Cod," says Jane Moyer, a busy consultant for high-tech companies in San Francisco. "I rent a cabin that's two blocks from the ocean and stay there for a week. The cabin has no phone or television. I don't get in my car; I don't listen to the radio and don't read newspapers. The sound of the waves is my only outside stimulation. I cook, I read, I walk on the beach. It's absolutely glorious." Back at work, Moyer says, she "sees things differently."[15]

The benefits of a vacation are numerous. Aside from relaxing and recharging, it's quite common, as Moyer said, to see old problems with new eyes after you return from a week of, say, skiing or scuba diving. "After a vacation, I'm more excited about getting back to work," one executive told me. "I'm enthusiastic and energized. My perceptions are sharper and I see things much clearer than when I left."[16]

Clarence Birdseye built a giant company and revolutionized the retail food industry from an insight he gained on a fishing trip. Noticing an Eskimo's fish frozen in the ice gave him the idea for frozen food. I guess that trip was worth the price.

So start taking what is owed to you in terms of your vacation. And leave your cell phone, pager, and your watch at home.

Up Time

Remember, taking a time-out, whether it's a five-minute break at the office or two weeks on a South Sea Island, isn't downtime. In fact, it is just the opposite. These breaks will reenergize your up time, increasing your creativity, productivity, and enthusiasm. You might even have some fun while you're at it.

Robert Foster, the CEO of GlobalRooms.com, a hospitality Internet company dealing with periods of high occupancy demand, adds that it is important to actually schedule time-outs or something else will come up that seems more important.

One of the first things you can do during a time-out is to focus on eliminating the things you are doing that prevent change and innovation and are causing you to work too damn hard. The next three chapters discuss ways of cutting down or cutting out the most common activities that waste an inordinate amount of time and energy.

))))➡ KEEP IN MIND
➡ Schedule "think time" every day.
➡ Spend time "out of touch."
➡ Incubation is necessary for inspiration and innovation.
➡ Creativity has a mind of its own.

[1] *Fast Company*, October 1998, p. 212.
[2] *Time*, 4 December 2000, p. 69.
[3] *Tom Peters Brand Everything Workbook*, 16 August 2000.
[4] *Fast Company*, 6 May 2000, p. 128.
[5] *Fortune*, 2 April 2001, p. 202.
[6] Joey Reiman, *Thinking for a Living*, (Marietta, Ga.: Longstreet, 1998), p. 30.
[7] *Time*, 4 December 2000, Special Section on Inventors.
[8] Kriegel, Robert J., and Marilyn H. Kriegel, *The C Zone* (New York: Doubleday, 1984).
[9] *Fast Company*, October 1999, p. 348.
[10] *Fast Company*, February/March 1999, p. 84.
[11] Ibid.
[12] *Fast Company*, October 1999, p. 348.
[13] *Sacramento Bee*, 25 June 2001, D5.
[14] *New York Times*, 1 November 1998, p. B2.
[15] *Fast Company*, May 2000, p. 108.
[16] Ibid.

CHAPTER 6

E-Mail Epidemic

One of the biggest causes of working too damn hard is that piece of technology that promised to help us communicate more effectively, work more efficiently, and cut down our workload. E-mail is like some wonder drug that promised dramatic results, but because of overdosing, it has begun to cause what it professed to cure. "People are using it for everything," one manager told me. "It's like an epidemic that's gotten out of control." Whenever I ask a group if they are getting a lot of e-mail, the response is a collective moan.

You know how it is. You arrive at the office, turn on your computer, and what do you hear? That cheerful, slightly mechanical voice announcing that "you've got mail." Doesn't that guy ever sleep?

"That's like the voice of doom," one manager told me, "because I know it means that for at least the next half hour or more I will be going through my e-mail. The worst part is that I am fresh and ready to go in the morning, but after I work through all my e-mail, I'm exhausted."

Andrea Gold, the president of Gold Stars Speakers Bureau, told me that sifting through her e-mail every morning typically takes an hour. "Some of it is important," she told me, "but much of it is information that I don't need. So sorting through it becomes a huge waste of time."

Do you look at your e-mails in the morning and think,

"Oh, good, here's something that's going to help"? Or "Egads! How am I ever going to get through them all?"

A manager from Microsoft told me that she received an average of over one hundred e-mails a day, and that three hundred wasn't rare. "I could spend the day just responding to them," she told me. "It's exhausting, debilitating, and infuriating."

"We're so wrapped up in sending e-mail to each other, we don't have time to be dealing with the outside," says Nathan Zeldes, Intel's computing productivity manager.[1] Employees of the semiconductor giant collectively average three million e-mails a day, with some people racking up as many as three hundred messages in one twenty-four-hour day.

A marketing director for one of the Big Five consulting companies told me that "I don't open my e-mail until about eleven A.M. If I opened it up first thing, I'd be spending most of my morning, which is my most creative time, just responding to e-mails."

The typical corporate e-mail user receives about thirty messages a day and spends more than two hours a day dealing with these messages, according to recent survey by Ferris Research.[2] This is up 50 percent from a year earlier. What's more, companies are projecting an increase in the next year of between 35 percent and 50 percent in the number of messages received. It's possible, therefore, that in 2002, employees will be spending four hours of their workday on e-mail. And a significant portion of this mounting e-mail volume is messages from colleagues who are within walking or even shouting distance of each other.

Jamie Rosen, the chairman and chief operating officer of Comet Systems, finds that "the more you use and respond to e-mail, the more of it you generate, so I'm spending more and more of my day on it." He is beginning to wonder if it is more of a burden than a benefit, lowering his productivity rather than boosting it. "I can't keep up and can't imagine how executives in larger companies do."[3]

TIME SAVER OR TIME WASTER?

Don't get me wrong. I'm not against e-mail. In fact, I'm a great proponent of it. Used properly, it is an incredibly effective and efficient tool that can dramatically cut down the time it takes to communicate information. It also saves paper and thus the cost of buying and storing the paper as well as the space and time it takes to file the paper.

The problem, as with many new tools, is that is it being misused, overused, and abused. People now tend to use it for everything, causing it to be an inefficient means of communication.

E-mail is often used to substitute for any face-to-face or even voice-to-voice communication. "The CEO of our company never leaves his office," the general manager of a large engineering company told me. "When he wants to communicate with me, boom! E-mail. And his office is only about twenty feet away."

Self-Perpetuating

One manager told me of a horror story (everyone seems to have one) that represented how self-perpetuating e-mail had become in their company. "It used to be that we'd have a meeting in which someone would recommend something and everyone would give feedback. Now the recommendation is e-mailed and everyone receiving it sends their responses, but not only to the sender, to everyone on the list. So now e-mails are buzzing back and forth to and from everyone involved in the decision. The result is that we're besieged by an epidemic of e-mails. And with all that e-mailing, what are the chances a decision ever gets implemented? Zilch! Please, I never thought I'd ask for this, but how about a short meeting?"

And then there are those people who call or leave a voice mail to ensure that you have received their e-mail. How about just asking for a reply if it's necessary, rather than wasting someone's time with yet another phone call or voice mail?

Paper Chase

One of the potential benefits of e-mail, aside from speed and saving time, is that it decreases the amount of paper we receive. But in some companies I work with—are you ready for this?—people not only send you e-mail but then send you a fax and an original copy of the same document. When I ask about this, it's always the same response: "We want to be double sure that people get the message." Why not simply ask for a response to the e-mail and forget the paper? "Never thought of that," one manager told me. That's precisely the problem. We get a new tool that has terrific potential, but when we're in a hurry, who has time to think about how to use it? So we abuse it.

Routing List from Hell

Did you ever get one of those e-mails in which you are one of a hundred names on a routing list that is three times as long as the message? The story behind this is usually that someone wants to ensure that he gets credit for his idea, or to cover his butt so that everyone knows he is still alive and doing something. Most of the recipients on the list have no need for the information. But there it sits waiting to be read and, of course, filed.

"On a typical day, I receive anywhere between one hundred and two hundred e-mails," a senior manager at Novell told me. "In most of those, I am in the middle of a routing list, which means I am not the intended recipient of that communication. But I still feel I have to go through all of them. What an incredible waste of time."

"I never read anything that is not sent directly to me," the general manager of a large manufacturing plant told me. "I can't afford to. I don't have the time. Whenever I see that I am on the routing list, I know it's not something that is important for me, so I immediately delete it. I always figure that if it is important for me to read, they'll send it to me directly."

A few months ago, Jamie Rosen told his seventy employees at Comet Systems that he didn't have time to read e-mails they wrote to other employees and copied to him. "I told them that if they really needed me to see something, they should send it directly to me or tell me face-to-face."[4]

Good advice. No routing lists. A good rule is to delete any e-mail, or any paperwork for that matter, that is not addressed to you directly. Many companies now ban routing lists. Brian Fugerre, the director of marketing and a partner at Deloitte Consulting, made his staff take a pledge to eliminate indiscriminate sending of e-mails, including "reply to all," responses and "copy universe" memos. A simple step is to get yourself removed from all distribution lists you don't really need to be on.

E-Mail Upmanship

There's another game going on that has to do with routing. It's called "A-List/E-Lists," according to David Brooks in a *New Yorker* magazine article.[5] Brooks describes it as a form of name-dropping in which an e-mail includes in its routing list people like the president of the company, a United States senator, a famous movie star, the Pope, and a best-selling author. None of whom the sender knows, of course. The e-mail isn't intended to communicate with any of these people, but merely to impress you.

The best thing to do when you receive one of these e-mail-upmanship missives is to just press Delete.

One Pagers

Keep your e-mail to one page. Limit it to the critical points. That will save everyone time and energy and will gain you lasting admiration and appreciation. Inform the recipients of your one pager where or how they can get support material if it is needed. I have found most managers, especially those at the top, usually don't want or need more than the headlines anyway. When possible, send a message that is only a subject line so recipients don't have to open it to read it.

Making It More Meaningful

Shelly Lazarus, the chair and CEO of advertising giant Ogilvy & Mather, thinks e-mail is important, but she reminds us, "There's no substitute for face-to-face. Something happens when you are in the room with people with whom you work, trying to solve a problem together or just listening to them. And the e-mail becomes more meaningful after the trip with the face-to-face."[6]

Mark McCormack, the premier sports agent in the country and the author of the best-selling book *What They Don't Teach You at Harvard Business School*, says that for something really important he would travel five thousand miles for a five-minute meeting.

Personal contact is a more powerful tool for inspiring and motivating employees. Even voice mail is better than e-mail for these purposes. "If you want to compliment a salesperson for doing a great job, you can communicate not just words, but emotion as well on the phone. This doesn't happen in e-mail,"[7] says Joseph Galli, former number two man at Black & Decker, president of Amazon, and now CEO of Vertical Net.

One of my rules is, don't send an e-mail if your proposed recipient sits nearby. Walk over to their office and give them the information. As Ms. Lazarus says, there's no substitute for face-to-face communication. And paraphrasing Mark McCormack, if something is real important, get off your butt and go see them. You don't want to be one of a zillion e-mails on someone's computer.

Jokes—It's Not So Funny

And how about all those jokes that get e-mailed? Don't get me wrong. I think we need more laughter and fun in the workplace. The problem is that most of the jokes I receive, like a recent one on kosher recipes, aren't that funny.

Another problem with these jokes is that they are usually unbelievably long. And by the time I have finished reading one, if I haven't already deleted it, I am usually bored. There is definitely nothing funny about the time wasted reading them.

An information technology manager at Kodak told me they did a study that found that the time their employees— over one hundred thousand—spent reading jokes, about eighteen seconds each, was costing the company over ten million dollars.

So save the jokes for the water cooler.

Thank-You Notes

Some people feel that they should respond when they get e-mail. So they send you back something like "Thanks for your e-mail" and maybe another line or two. Sure, it may be polite and your parents told you to respond and send thank-you notes. But even a short response and thanks takes a couple of minutes. And if you have fifteen of them, well, you get the idea.

Some e-mails obviously need a response, but many are just information and don't. So take a risk and don't respond. Your mother may not approve, but she's not on the other end anyway. Focus on efficiency, not politeness. The Ferris Research report advises managers to avoid back-and-forth replies such as "Thank you" and "OK."[8]

Sorting ... Sort Of

John Wanamaker, one of America's pioneering retailers, once said about advertising something that could have been said about e-mail. "I know half of it doesn't work. The problem is that I don't know which half."

One way to solve the problem that Wanamaker described

is to use the e-mail subject box to identify different categories. One high-tech organization uses numbers from 1 to 5 to delineate the level of urgency, with 5 being the most important. Another uses different-colored flags, with red the most urgent.

You can also use a code in the subject slot, identifying the type of e-mail it is. An example could be:

FYI—for your information
RAL—read at your leisure
URGNT—read at once
NRN—no response necessary
RR—reply requested
FYI/CMB—for your information, covering my butt
HAHA—joke

E-Mail Etiquette

The Lakewood Report on Technology and Training says that fewer than 5 percent of organizations offer training on how to use e-mail, and the bulk of this training focuses on how to use the software. They suggest that investing an hour or two on e-mail etiquette training will dramatically affect the character and usefulness of hundreds of thousands of e-mails. They offer training modules on such subjects such as how to write a subject line that tells it all, sending e-mails that don't require a response, and when you should just pick up the phone.

Whatever you do, do something to stop the e-mail epidemic in your organization. Make the best use of this potentially efficient and effective tool by learning to use, not abuse or be used by it. You'll save an incredible amount of time. Time that you can use to think.

))⟩➡ KEEP IN MIND

➠ Never e-mail someone who is within shouting distance.
➠ Save the jokes for the water cooler.

➠ Eliminate routing lists; don't read cc'd e-mail.
➠ Don't leave voice mail to check that your e-mail has been received.
➠ Forget "Thanks you's" and "OK's."

[1] *Fast Company*, March 2001, p. 56.
[2] *San Francisco Examiner*, 8 October 2000.
[3] Ibid.
[4] Ibid., p. J-3.
[5] *New Yorker*, 13 September 1999, p. 50.
[6] *New York Times*, 10 October 1999, p. B3.
[7] *San Francisco Examiner*, 8 October 2000, p. J-3.
[8] Ibid.

CHAPTER 7

Meeting Mania

When was the last time you made a phone call to someone and actually got him on the line? Where is everybody? What's going on? Isn't anyone ever at his desk? Nope. They're all in meetings. Staff meetings, status meetings, client meetings, goal-setting meetings, strategy sessions. You name it and there is a meeting for it. Most people are spending more than half their workday in meetings.

TIME DRAINS

The biggest complaint I hear from the stressed-out and overworked is "I can't get any work done. All I do is go to meetings." One manager told me that he used to get to the office early when it was quiet and stay a little late to get control of his desk. "But now we have meetings as early as seven A.M. and others that go through dinner."

Jill Marshall, the dean of a major educational institution, explained, "I go to one meeting and come out with a bunch of action items. But before I get a chance to work on my To Do list from that meeting, I have to go to another meeting where I accumulate more action items for my To Do list. Sure, some of the meetings are good and worthwhile, but the real problem is that there are so many of them that I don't have a chance to process what happened and to do any follow-up on the ideas that come out of them. As a result, my To Do list keeps getting longer and my Done list shorter."

"We have way too many meetings," says Joe Weller, the CEO and chairman of Nestlé USA. "Meetings waste time and sap people's energy. They slow us down. So far I've been polite about breaking them up. But this year I won't tolerate them."[1]

It would be fine if these meetings were productive, but in most cases, there are *too many* meetings, that last *too long* and accomplish *too little*. Survey after survey shows that meetings are rarely a source of great ideas or innovative thinking and that most are a huge waste of time. Most people are spending half their workday sitting in these gatherings. Imagine if those hours were well spent. Spent wisely. Spent creatively. We'd all be home in time for dinner and to play with our kids or get in a round of golf before dark.

Earless

One reason that meetings seem to go on forever and use up valuable time and money is a lack of ears. Most people don't listen to one another. They just sit there planning what to say and waiting for their chance to say it.

Michael Begeman, the manager of 3M's Meeting Network and an authority on the subject, describes most business meetings thus: "You could take the people out and replace them with radios blaring at each other and you wouldn't have changed very much. That's what most meetings are like. People wait for the person who's speaking to take a breath, so they can jump into the space and talk. The quality of communications in most meetings is roughly comparable to the quality or arguments that you used to have with your ten-year-old brother."[2]

No Surprises

Surprises are one of the causes of those overly long Excedrin headache sessions. Recently I, along with several other consultants, attended a meeting of one of our clients, an Internet start-up company. The purpose of the meeting was to develop a sales and marketing strategy. We had all prepared our thoughts and recommendations. When we arrived, however, *surprise!*—the president distributed his new business plan. The project manager then handed out her agenda, which consisted of many areas discussed in detail in the business plan, which, of course, none of us had read.

The result was that time had to be spent clarifying issues that were in the business plan. A colleague muttered, "He must have thought we were psychic and we could hold the plan to our foreheads and magically know the contents." The meeting, which lasted two and a half hours with little accomplished, would have taken about half that time and been much more productive had they sent out the agenda and the business plan in advance.

It's important to bring people up to speed prior to a meeting. Don't waste your time, and theirs, by doing it *during* the meeting. To save time and make your meeting more productive, have a clear agenda, get it to people in advance, and stick to it. If you're going to change the agenda, change your meeting.

Save your surprises for your kid's birthday, which, if you shorten your meetings, you'll have time to attend.

COSTLY

Most meetings are not only a waste of time, but a waste of money. Next time you are sitting in on one, calculate everyone's approximate salary for that period of time. Then ask yourself if that meeting is worth it. One of the major consulting companies was holding weekly, hour-long, worldwide teleconferences for all of their consultants. This practice was discontinued when it was discovered that this nonbillable time cost more than $1.5 million a month.

A staffer working for Mayor Rudy Giuliani's New York

City government examined the cost of meetings that the ten city managers were regularly attending. Each individual was spending approximately 1.5 hours in each meeting and attending four each day. The salary of these top managers was $90,000, which breaks down to $400 a day or $53 an hour. Each meeting, therefore, was costing the city approximately $795.00, with a daily cost of $3,200 for the four meetings. Multiply this by five days and the cost is $16,000 a week, or $832,000 a year. So the meetings for just ten managers were costing the city close to a million bucks in salary alone. How much do your meetings cost? And what is the return on that investment?

MAKING MEETINGS WORK

Below are several techniques to make your meetings more productive and less time consuming.

The 50 Percent Solution

Meetings follow the law of physics for hot air—of which there's usually no shortage. They expand to fill the space available. So shorten them! At a major New York advertising agency, everyone agreed that the weekly hour-and-a-half staff meeting was much too long, so they shortened it to forty-five minutes. It worked! People arrived on time, cut the premeeting chitchat, and stuck to the agenda. Everyone agreed that they got more done in less time. The manager then sent out a memo stating that no meeting should run more than forty-five minutes.

I have found the 50 percent solution—cutting the duration and frequency of meetings in half—to be incredibly effective. A weekly hour-long staff meeting is then shortened to a biweekly half hour. Pay attention to the law of physics; limit the time of your meetings and you'll limit the empty talk and get more real work done.

Vertical Meetings

Another problem is that people come to a meeting and "take a load off." Companies like Johnson & Johnson, Equitable Life, and Corning Glass have drastically cut their meeting times by *removing the chairs*! The average time for these vertical meetings was a power-packed half hour.

Sparrow Time

At a managers' conference for Michigan's Sparrow Health Care, people were complaining both about the number of meetings they had to attend and how much time they took. But one person stated that the real problem wasn't the number of meetings but that the meetings operated on Sparrow time.

Some new kind of clock? I wondered. Nope. Sparrow time meant that meetings usually started about fifteen minutes late. So the people who arrived early or even on time had to sit around and schmooze and fret, waiting for the latecomers.

Sparrow time doesn't only happen in Michigan. In companies that I have worked with throughout the United States, the difference between the stated starting time of the meeting and the actual starting time is usually between ten and fifteen minutes. One meeting planner for a major utility told me not to worry if I arrived late because of my airline schedule: "We always start meetings late around here," she said.

"What's the big deal—it's only ten minutes," you're thinking. You're right, it's not a big deal . . . *if you go to only one meeting a day*. But if, like most people, you are going to four or five meetings, you're talking about losing an hour. That's an hour you could be spending doing some real work or at home with your family.

Not only do you lose valuable time when meetings start late, but you honor tardiness and devalue punctuality. Starting late also sends a message of looseness and lack of rigor.

Soon it's not only that meetings are running later, but deadlines are missed, reports are late; "Hey, what's the big deal, it's only a day."

Make Them Pay

One solution to solving the tardiness factor is to make the latecomers pay—literally. A large manufacturer fined people a dollar for every minute they were late. But that was chump change, so it was raised to three dollars per minute. It worked wonderfully (they used the money for charitable donations). At another company, the door was locked to latecomers. If you didn't get to the meeting on time, you didn't get in.

Often the boss is the culprit. In a large metropolitan hospital, the chief operating officer was routinely fifteen to twenty minutes late for their weekly meeting. This frustrated and annoyed the forty-five doctors and nurses on his senior staff. One time, after fifteen minutes and no sign of the boss, they were so angry that they left. This infuriated the boss when he finally did arrive. Same thing happened the following week, but this time the group left a note detailing the cost in terms of people's time that his tardiness was costing the hospital. He got the message. *Caution: Use this strategy only if everyone walks. Don't walk alone.*

Habit Meetings

A human resources manager at one of the largest steel companies told me that they had many "habit meetings," which, he explained, "are the kind that we'd been scheduling regularly for years. We seem to keep having them more out of habit than because of any specific purpose. It's like the emperor has no clothes. Everyone knows that these meetings aren't accomplishing much, but no one is willing to say anything."

Make sure you are clear about the purpose of a meeting before you go. And if there isn't a good reason for the meeting, cancel it.

TIME FOR TRUST

Meetings don't need to be all business. Sure, you want to get things accomplished, but there's a social aspect that is important to include in meetings and that is not a waste of time. Trust is a critical factor in developing teamwork, communication, and creativity. And trust is developed by people feeling connected to each other. A little time to socialize can go a long way toward developing successful teams and making meetings productive. But too much of a good thing and you end up with the opposite.

Schedule a little "hang" time to get people relaxed, comfortable, and present and then get on with it.

➠ **KEEP IN MIND**
- ➠ Cut the duration and frequency of your meetings in half.
- ➠ Charge latecomers; bar the door.
- ➠ Keep 'em standing.
- ➠ No surprises—know the purpose of the meeting in advance.
- ➠ Don't go to meetings that aren't important.

[1] *Fast Company*, June 2001, p. 170.
[2] *Fast Company*, April 1999, p. 206.

CHAPTER 8

Out-of-the-Box Meetings

After you have pared down your meetings to a precious few, there are ways to stimulate creativity, innovation, and out-of-the-box thinking in the ones you have left. Here are some guidelines.

CREATIVE ENVIRONMENT

Fresh ideas rarely emerge in a stale environment. It is hard to think out of the box when you are sitting in a room that resembles one. When I began working in advertising, the creative department was king. These were the tradition-busting old days of the Volkswagen "Think Small" campaign, Avis boasting that they were number two and trying harder, Braniff telling you that if you've got it, flaunt it, and Levy's Rye Bread claiming that you didn't have to be Jewish to eat their product.

The offices of the copywriters and art directors in those days looked more like art galleries than places of business. Entering the creative department was an event. All kinds of art, masks, sculptures, and quotations decorated the walls, which were often painted in wild colors and patterns. Music from opera to rock blared.

All that changed when a new marketing-oriented president took over. The offices in the creative department then became uniform boxes, and there were restrictions on what you could put on the wall. This shift in emphasis also brought a shift in product. "It's dullsville around here now, and you can see it in the ads," one creative director sadly told me.

Thinkubators

"If you want people to be creative, you have to put them in an environment that lets their imagination soar,"[1] says Gerald Haman, the founder of Creative Solutions Network, which helped Kraft develop new pasta, cheese, and pizza products and helped Peoples Energy Corp. find new uses for natural gas. To stimulate people's imagination, Haman created a Thinkubator, which is a combination rec room and art gallery filled with fun stuff like furniture in the shape of a lightbulb, a conch shell, and a bright red pair of lips. There's a great sound system with five hundred CDs, and a Wall of Wonder displaying the skylines of thirty cities. "There's a definite correlation between people's comfort level and their creativity level,"[2] Haman says. So shoes are discarded in the Thinkubator, and Haman has even been known to slice the necktie of an uptight client.

Off-Site and Out of Mind

This doesn't mean that you have to create a loony-bin or frat-house environment in order to generate creative ideas. But it's important to get away from the office—away from the phones, faxes, pagers, and constant interruptions. When meeting in an office environment, people's minds keep returning to that phone call they have to make, the report they should be doing, or the e-mail they have to answer. The aura of business taking place all around pervades the meeting and inhibits creativity.

Meeting off-site in an unusual environment is much more conducive to creativity. The further your meeting is from your work, both physically and mentally, the better the results. Wherever you go, make sure phone calls and beepers are verboten. The minute the cell phone rings or the beeper beeps, people's minds revert to business as usual. In Finland, the home of Nokia, over 90 percent of the population have cell phones, yet there are billboards telling you to "Remember your phone has an off button." This is great advice for us all.

Fun

There is a direct correlation between fun and creativity. John Cleese once interviewed the Dalai Lama and asked him, "Why it is that in Tibetan Buddhism they all laugh so much?" The Dalai Lama told him, very seriously, that "the laughter is very helpful in teaching and indeed in political negotiations, because when people laugh it is easier for them to admit new ideas into their mind."[3]

Laughter involves the creative right side of the brain. Playing games and offering activities that help people relax, have fun, and experience a sense of teamwork encourages breakthrough thinking. It's tough to come up with innovative ideas when you are tense and uptight.

One of the rules a Texas engineering company has for its brainstorming sessions is that everyone has to wear a funny shirt or a ridiculous costume. The chief operating officer told me, "It's tough to take things too seriously when you are at a meeting and the guy sitting next to you is wearing a toga." It's also unlikely that creativity will be stifled by a boss wearing reindeer antlers.

It's especially important to introduce some games at the start of a creativity session in order to loosen people up. The best exercises are those that involve physical activity. The more outrageous the game, the less inhibited and the more creative people become.

Trust

Playing games and having fun also helps people get to know each other on a more personal basis. This helps create the trust that is essential for creativity. If people don't trust the environment or their teammates, they will be more inhibited and the creative juices won't flow. A good way to establish this trust is to let it be known that nothing is repeated outside of the meeting.

Food

One of the least productive times in any meeting is after a group has had a big meal. All the blood and energy goes to the stomach, which is not where creativity is generated. On the other hand, when you are in a meeting and hungry, guess what you are focused on? While hunger may be a good motivator, it's not terrific for generating creative ideas on subjects other than food.

So feed people snacks instead of big meals. Have an abundance of cheese, veggies, dips, fruit, candy, and herbal energy boosters. At Creative Solutions' Thinkubator, they have cookies in the shape of lightbulbs. At Digital Pilot, a Dallas-based software company, they have biweekly snack sessions whose purpose is to breed a bold, innovative, risk-taking culture and to encourage radical thinking. They start the meeting with milk and cookies and even give candy bars to people with the boldest ideas.

SLOWER IS BETTER

One of the biggest inhibitors to creativity is a lack of time. It's difficult to come up with original ideas when you feel hurried and harried. Since everyone is rushed these days and trying to do more in less time, the natural tendency is to solve a problem quickly in order to get on to the next meeting or project. The result of this mentality is premature closure—going with the first idea that comes up. The problem is that it's often the second or even third idea that is the barn burner. But if you are in a hurry, you'll never get past the first.

Creativity doesn't happen on demand. In fact, quite the opposite. "Slower is better. You can't hurry great ideas,"[4] says Joey Reiman, founder of Brighthouse, an ideation corporation that has won literally hundreds of awards for creativity. As I mentioned, the best ideas often happen when you least expect them, when you are sleeping, driving, or exercising. During these times, your unconscious mind is percolating, sifting, sorting, and making connections you aren't even aware of.

And then—aha!—the lightbulb hits. "One way to arrive at a great idea is by letting yourself be slower than everyone else,"[5] says Reiman, whose company has developed break-through ideas for clients such as Coca-Cola, Home Depot, Georgia Pacific, and Delta Airlines.

On the Other Hand

Urgency creates motivation. Without some deadline, other priorities will grab people's attention, and creative ideas that you're hoping to implement will be pushed so far back on the back burner that they'll never come to fruition. So have a deadline and an action plan that gets people motivated but not harried and hassled. In other words, keep them moving but don't rush them.

BE OUTRAGEOUS

If you want to instill out-of-the-box thinking, it's important to start out being as outrageous as possible. Creativity can be squashed by getting "realistic" too quickly. Don't edit your thoughts. Anything goes. The real breakthrough idea may sound totally crazy at first. But by giving it a little spin or twist, it can often turn out to be a major breakthrough.

"The best ideas usually sound absolutely insane at first, so we don't want people to be editing their thoughts,"[6] says Jeff

Charney, the senior vice president of marketing for Kaufman & Broad, the home builders known for their innovative marketing.

To paraphrase Albert Einstein, "If at first an idea doesn't sound absurd, there's no hope for it."[7]

The first part of any brainstorming meeting should be a no-holds-barred session. Defer any judgments about whether something is realistic. You also can't tell how seemingly unrelated ideas can turn into an unexpected breakthrough. And remember when you are brainstorming that there are no bad ideas.

One very creative group does try to come up with as many off-the-top-of-your-head ideas as quickly as possible. Their goal is to shoot for 150 ideas in thirty to forty-five minutes.

You can also start by playing games and doing activities that exercise creative, right-brain thinking. I often ask a group what animal their product or service represents. The answers to this question have helped shape many ideas. One company viewed their service as an octopus with many tentacles reaching out to the customer. Another game is to have people pretend they are aliens and have never seen the product.

After this type of brainstorming, it's important to give people a chance to mull the ideas over and let them percolate. I often have people take a walk by themselves. The next step, which may even be in a next meeting, is to bring the blue-sky ideas down to earth, to turn them into something that can be implemented. But remember, you'll get mediocre results if you try to get to reality too quickly.

STOKE THE FIRES AND BURN THE PLATFORMS

Motivation is critical for coming up with creative ideas. Get your team excited about the possibilities of what "could be" if you develop a new solution to an old problem or come up with a breakthrough new idea. Personal opportunities and exciting possibilities are great motivators. People will naturally become more motivated when there is something personal at stake. Stoke your group's fire and get them excited by talking about the opportunities that exist for them.

Another way to motivate people is to discuss the consequences of resisting change. There are many examples in every industry of companies that became dinosaurs by standing pat, resting on laurels, and playing by old rules. You can use some of these examples to generate a sense of urgency and get people off the dime. But though fear may be a good short-term motivator for lighting a fire, it is not conducive to creativity. A scared person is not a creative person. It's important to turn the fear into excitement.

BEWARE ATTENTION HOGS

Every meeting has them: the people who seem to take up all the space, do most of the talking, and hog center stage. It's important to get people talking, but if one person dominates the meeting, it will often intimidate others. It's often the quiet, shy person who will come up with the best idea. But if they feel intimidated, they'll just sit there like a clam.

You don't know where the best ideas will come from or who will come up with them. *New York Times* best-selling novelist Larry Bond says, "The vital thing to understand is that nobody has a monopoly on good ideas and that almost any idea can be improved."[8] With this in mind, it's important to make sure that everyone has a chance to speak. Pay attention to the quiet people. Make an easy entry for them, don't pressure them or they'll clam up and say nothing.

Many people don't want to say what they are thinking for fear of sounding stupid and making a fool of themselves. Setting the tone for a fun, relaxed, anything-goes atmosphere will make it easier for these cautious types to open up. You might even hold a contest for the zaniest ideas. One way for the leader to encourage the quiet people to get involved is to be the first to come out with some crazy, off-the-wall idea.

A RICH TAPESTRY

The more different points of view you have in a meeting, the better off you are. Ideas will be limited if you have all middle-aged, middle-class accountants or all young, hip marketers on a team. Try to get a rich diversity of jobs, experience, background, and culture. Broadening the variety of people you have in the meeting will result in a wider range of perspective and viewpoints. People coming from different jobs, cultures, and backgrounds will look at a problem with different eyes and see different possibilities. The marketer will look at a problem in one way, while the factory supervisor will see it totally differently. And that's what you want.

⫸ KEEP IN MIND

To stimulate creativity in meetings:
➠ Get away from your work environment.
➠ Create trust and get everyone involved.
➠ Have fun and be outrageous before you get realistic.
➠ Don't go with the first idea.
➠ No negatives.
➠ Diversity—get a wide variety of experiences and backgrounds.

[1] *Fast Company*, April 1999, p. 44.
[2] Ibid.
[3] *Fortune*, 6 July 1998, p. 203.
[4] Joey Reiman, conversation with the author, 5 June 2000.
[5] Ibid.
[6] *Fast Company*, June 1999, p. 72.
[7] *Fortune*, 12 April 1999, p. 165.
[8] Larry Bond, *Day of Wrath* (New York: Warner Books, 1998), Author's note.

CHAPTER 9

Paperless—Ha!

R emember the promise of the information age—the paperless office? Know anyone that has one? It's those reports and reviews, forecasts and forms, that eat up a large percentage of your time at work and cause most of us to work too damn hard, too damn long, with too damn little to show for it. Though that mound of paper sitting in front of you seems harmless, it steals time, saps energy, costs money, and prevents you from doing things that add value to your work or your life.

Many executives I have consulted with assured me that their organizations were just about paperless. Yet when I entered their office, the piles of paper were so high I couldn't even see them sitting there. What's that, I wondered, camouflage?

How's this for paperless: Shipments of paper to American industry in the last ten years have increased by more than 50 percent! We're getting much more than we need and more than we can read. It seems impossible to catch up no matter how many hours we spend at work.

The head of human resources at a major financial services company told me that a recent study their company did showed that despite all their advances in information technology, the amount of paper they now receive has not been reduced from the amount received ten years ago. "In fact, it has increased," she told me. "People don't trust the technology.

They're printing out their e-mail and filing it. Many of them even send hard copies of e-mails to insure their message is received. What a waste of time!"

VALUELESS

The new CFO for a major corporation, under the promise of anonymity, estimated the following time allocations for his financial department: 15 percent on various forms of statutory compliance reporting, such as audits, tax, ERISA; 20 percent on ongoing or one-time project analysis that clearly adds substantial value to line organization efforts; 65 percent on paperwork for maintaining, updating, and operating internal financial systems that adds *little if any value* to line organization efforts. I bet if more people were honest they would admit to similar allocations of time.

The Pleasures of Paper Pushing

A three-star general told me that many of his sergeants actually loved paperwork. "Yep," he said, "they prefer the paperwork to the people work. These types get a cup of coffee, go into their office, close the door, and start in on the paper, and you don't see them for the rest of the day. They're happy as a clam. Paperwork is comfortable. It's something they know how to do. Hell, most of it is routine stuff. What's really important is working with people problems, which is much more difficult and gets shelved."

Think about it. Paper has a beginning and an end. You start out with a mountain on your desk and gradually whittle it down to a molehill and feel a sense of the satisfaction that comes with completion. People work, on the other hand, is far more complex and always a work in progress.

The kicker came about a year ago when I ran into the general at a conference. He had retired from the Army and was now the chairman of a Fortune 100 company. "You know," he told me, "I see the same thing happening in corporate America as in the Army. Loads of managers that would rather do paperwork than get out in the trenches where the action is."

Readerless Paper

Want to know what happens with much of that paper you work so hard to get right and finish on time? Nothing. Much of it is filed unread. And a great deal of it ends up in the round file. When supervisors at one of U.S. Steel's main mills complained about a daily operational report that was deemed critical, the general manager admitted he never read it.

Reports going unread is a common occurrence. One of the major peeves of the executives at a large retail chain in the Southeast was a monthly financial report that had to be sent to the directors. It wasn't the one-page summary that they complained about. It was all the support material that had to accompany it as documentation. "Oh, I never read all that backup stuff," the chairman said. "It would take too much time. I round-file that part of the report. I figure if there's something I don't understand on the summary, I'll give you a call."

Then there was the bimonthly report one of the Big Five accounting firms sent to all the partners and clients that was costing a whopping $750K annually. Working with the CFO and his group, we cut down a considerable amount of the cost when I noticed an entry of $40K for FedEx. "Why not send it second-day FedEx?" I asked. "That would save almost half the expense, and I'm sure these reports probably don't get read the day they are received."

The CFO looked at me with an incredulous stare and said, "You obviously don't know this business. Not read the first day? Hell, I bet most of these reports never get read at all."

Duplicate Efforts

One of the causes of the plethora of paper is that in many companies, several departments pump out the same information. When Chris Higgins, a senior vice president of Bank of America, joined the bank, he found 130 projects waiting for him. One of his first jobs was to have each project leader write the name of every project on which he or she was working on one side of an index card. On the other side of the card, they were told to write a short description of the project. The result was that 30 percent of the projects were duplicating the work of other projects.

At a major department store, the receiving department had to check and fill out a form detailing the contents of each incoming shipment. This same procedure was repeated by the merchandising department when the shipment was sent upstairs. And, of course, the accounting department also did it to check that the vendor's bill matched the shipment. Three departments replicating the same report.

REVIEWING REVIEWS

Everybody hates performance reviews. Managers hate doing them and the staff hates getting them. What's more, they're always at least two to three weeks late and put at the bottom of the To Do pile. Why? Because no one sees much value in them.

When I tell companies to eliminate these reviews, they respond in a panic, "But how are we going to let people know how they are doing? It's the basis for helping them improve and giving raises and the information goes into their folders."

Feedback Isn't a Piece of Paper

The bottom line is that the boss isn't doing his job if people don't know how they are doing on a *daily* basis. Feedback is essential for people to know how they are doing—and the quicker they get it, the more it will help them to improve, shore up weak points, and keep growing.

But the best feedback is not a piece of paper that people receive once a quarter. It is a pat on the back right after they have done well. Or a tip or word of advice when they haven't. "Anyone who equates delivering feedback with filling out forms has lost the battle for smart appraisal before it's begun," says Kelly Allan, a consultant whose clients include Boeing, Paramount Pictures, and IBM. "If you use forms as the basis for a meeting about performance, you change only one thing, what might have been a natural, helpful conversation into an awkward inspection."[1]

In other words, if Sarah screws up on something, let her know right away and help her to learn how to do it better. Don't wait till the end of the quarter to gunny-sack her. Feedback will be of value only if it is constant and continual. So save time and paper and make feedback immediate and personal.

Rally Round the Fire

At an executive meeting of a major packaging company, a review of key company policies resulted in a rally and bonfire. All the outdated, useless policy manuals fueled the bonfire. The company, Glenroy Inc., then reinvented these policies. But not performance reviews. "When people find out we don't have formal reviews, it drives them crazy. They don't understand how we can run the business," said Michael Dean, the executive vice president. "Leaders here provide people with feedback. But the way for it to be effective is on a day-to-day, minute-by-minute basis, not twice a year."[2]

JUST STOP DOING IT

Xerox used to have a process for evaluating employees in which everyone had to fill out reams of paperwork about their one-, three-, and five-year goals. Chris Turner, who had created Xerox's innovative learning laboratories, thought the process was absurd and useless, so he just stopped doing them.

Eventually everyone on the team stopped. Turner later got a call from someone in human resources who admitted that only thirty-five percent of all Xerox's employees were complying with this process. Turner told the HR people that everyone knew that being promoted had nothing to do with those forms. Pretty soon after that conversation, Xerox canned the forms thus saving the paper and their employees' valuable time.

Burning and Dumping

A major paper problem comes from an obsession with rules, policies, and procedures. When Jack Welch took over General Electric, the company was run by a set of its famous blue books. These five thick volumes, which provided guidance on just about everything, had been written by some of America's best thinkers, including Peter Drucker. The inherent message of these tomes to the managers "was that you don't have to think. The thinking has been done for you probably by people who are smarter than you."[3]

Welch burned the books and shifted toward empowering his managers to make more decisions on their own.

At Sears, managers were announcing new programs almost weekly. And store managers, already overburdened, were becoming frustrated with the constant barrage of mail from headquarters. To make the point, one executive showed up at a meeting with a wheelbarrow overflowing with a month's worth of memos, surveys, videos, and other communiqués and dumped the whole load on the floor.[4]

Ignoring

Anthropologist, psychoanalyst, and management scholar Michael Maccoby advises employees to discern which demands are truly worth heeding. "Many leaders often give subordinates many more orders than they can possibly execute. Ignore the requests that don't make sense," says Maccoby, "Forget about them. They will."[5]

The executive vice president for a major telecommunications company showed me a survey of the organization that revealed that managers were receiving over eighty-four hours of incoming messages a week. More than 80 percent of that was paper. His strategy was to divide all his incoming mail into three piles. First were the correspondences that weren't directed to him, but that he was copied on. He would send these back to the people who sent them, requesting that they never cc him again. The second pile was things that were urgent. He handled these immediately.

The third pile was less urgent material that he could later attend to when he had time, which, of course, was never.

"So what did you do with that pile?" I asked.

"I just throw it out," he told me.

"That sounds too glib," I told him.

"No," he told me. "If it isn't urgent, I chuck it, because I know when the issue becomes urgent, I will be sent another message. And I'll put that one on my To Do file and get it done."

PUT THE PAPER ON A DIET

Most of the paperwork you are doing today was developed years ago. Check it out to see which parts are outdated and can be eliminated or condensed. Putting your reports on a diet will probably make them much easier to read (if they are read) and save you lots of time writing and researching.

A major high-tech company required each of its divisions to send a ten-column monthly financial report to the executive committee. One division felt this was a huge waste of time and proposed cutting out two of the columns containing information everyone agreed was no longer relevant. They then sent the report in with eight columns, while all the other twenty divisions were still sending ten.

They got no response.

Feeling confident from their success, they eliminated two other columns because that information could be easily found on the Internet. They then sent out the report with six columns. When they again got no response, one person replied, "Maybe there's no one out there."

The following month they decided to find out and didn't send the report at all. Once again they got no response. For the next three months they didn't send out the report.

Finally they sent it out with four columns and called it the quarterly report. Keep in mind that all the other divisions were still sending out their monthly report with ten columns. Their quarterly report got a response. In red pencil the chairman wrote, "Great report! Simple. Clear. Keep up the good work!"

One Page

One rule mentioned in the chapter on e-mail is even more important with paperwork: No report, no proposal, no memo should be longer than one page. When I managed a Procter & Gamble account for Young & Rubicam, the advertising agency, the rule was that you couldn't send anything to them that was longer than one page, including the annual budget proposal, which involved advertising expenditures of tens of millions of dollars. You could have lots of support and backup materials, but all the points, the rationale, the background, and anything else of importance had to be on that one page.

Many writers act as if they are getting paid by the pound, adding lots of fat to impress the reader. But what they are really doing is frustrating the reader who hasn't the time or energy to go through all the material. It's a lot easier to write five or ten pages than it is one. Honing down your thoughts to one page is a great discipline for crystallizing your thinking. It forces you to determine what is important, what isn't, and how to state your case clearly and simply.

One of Winston Churchill's rules was said to be that nothing sent to him could be more than one page. "If you can't say it on one page, you don't know what you are talking about." That's wisdom we can all use.

De-Layering

Another huge time-waster is all the different levels people have to go through to get something approved. Managers in many companies with $50,000-plus budgets often have to get four signatures for a $100 piece of software or a travel chit. It often costs more money to get the approvals than it would have to purchase the needed equipment or go on the trip. Not to mention the hassles and time lost while waiting, as well as the demoralizing feeling of being treated like a young child waiting for his parents' OK to sleep over at a friend's house.

At an executive briefing for a major insurance company, the CFO proudly related that only $3 million of the $13 million allocated for employee awards and recognition had been spent. "Picked up $10 million on that one," the CFO crowed.

I later discovered that managers had to get five approvals in order to give a reward. "Every time I try to get some of the reward money for our best people," one of the middle managers told me, "I get the third degree from top management and lectures about budget and expenses. It's just not worth it." It didn't surprise me that the turnover rate in that company was 40 percent higher than the industry average.

Making people jump through hoops to get approval not only takes a huge amount of time, it indicates that you don't trust them. When people don't feel trusted, their motivation decreases, resulting in poor performance. If you don't trust them, they shouldn't have a big budget in the first place. And do you really want to have to read all those requests for approvals anyway?

CLEARING THE DECKS

My former editor, Susan Suffes, told me that her company gave its employees a half day off on Fridays in the summer. "The strange thing," Suffes confided, "is that I seemed to get as much work done on those half days as I did on my regular full day."

When I related this story to other companies that had these summer half days, many people had the same experience.

"How does this happen?" I always ask.

A manager at Abbott Labs told me, "I start by clearing the decks for action."

"Meaning?" I asked.

"I put aside all the stuff that doesn't have to be done and concentrate on what does. I also stop schmoozing in the halls and that kind of stuff," she told me.

"But what happens to the stuff that you put aside? Doesn't it catch up and choke you on Monday?" I inquired.

With a smile, she shrugged and said, "I don't know, it just sort of disappears. I usually end up not doing it. And what I've noticed is that no one seems to notice. Learning to clear the decks for action had been the best time management system I have ever used."

➠ **KEEP IN MIND**
➠ Nothing more than one page.
➠ Eliminate duplication.
➠ Burn rulebooks, purge performance reviews, use procedure manuals for doorstops.
➠ When in doubt, chuck it out.

[1] *Fast Company*, September 1998, p. 147.
[2] Ibid.
[3] *Fortune*, 27 November 1999, p. 187.
[4] *New York Times*, 15 January 1998, p. C3.
[5] *New York Times*, 30 January 2000, p. B13.

CHAPTER 10

Think Like a Beginner

L earning to think like a beginner is one of the most effective ways to reinvent your game. Experience, information, and expertise are obviously valuable, but to develop innovative solutions and spot new opportunities, it is essential to think more like a beginner than an expert. In his classic book *Zen Mind, Beginner's Mind,* Zen master Shunryu Suzuki writes, "In the beginner's mind there are many possibilities. In the expert's mind there are few. A beginner's mind is ready for anything. It is open to anything."[1]

A beginner is not as attached to the way it's always been done and won't spend a great deal of time beating dead horses or feeding sacred cows. The beginner's mind is more open to new ideas and possibilities and brings a fresh perspective into any situation. A beginner doesn't have preconceived notions about the way something should be done and approaches new situations with curiosity—perhaps the most important quality for innovative thinking. This type of thinking opens the mind to things that ordinarily wouldn't capture your attention.

Some of the best ideas come from people who know the least about a specific operation. Kozo Osborne, the managing director of Sony's audio group that developed such innovative products as the Walkman and Discman CD, said, "If you are designing something new, give it to the rookies."[2]

EXPERT'S THINKING

The biggest stumbling block to innovation and finding new solutions to old problems is the automatic reliance on experts. Conventional thinking values experience. Got a problem? Call in the consultant who is an expert in your field. But expertise comes from experience that comes from *the past.*

The CEO of a major supermarket chain was puzzled by his company's loss of volume and market share. "I don't understand it," he told me. "The economy is good, we have prime locations and terrific stores that offer the customer lots of choices and good service. One of our strengths is our management team. They really know the supermarket business. Most of our managers have been here on average over twenty-five years." Bingo!

Experts like the supermarket managers often rely on yesterday's solutions to solve today's problems. But with change happening so rapidly, relying on a strategy like this can put you out of business. Being steeped in experience deludes people into thinking they have the answer or know the right way to do things. This attitude closes their minds to new ideas and possibilities. "There's nothing worse than people who are full of themselves, who huff and puff and aren't curious," GE chief Jack Welch says. "If you aren't curious, you become arrogant. And that's the road to disaster."[3]

"In most companies, strategy is the preserve of the old guard," writes best-selling author Gary Hamel. "The same ten people talking to the same ten people year after year. No wonder the strategies that emerge are dull. What, after all, can the top twenty or thirty executives in a company learn from each other? Their positions are so well rehearsed they can finish each other's sentences."[4]

History Lesson

I first became aware of the danger of listening to the experts who were steeped in experience when managing a Procter & Gamble account for Young & Rubicam. Whenever we wanted to try a new promotion or advertising strategy, the market research director, who had worked on Procter accounts forever, could give us the history of any type of promotion, tell us the right one to use, and predict the results.

Since this marketing guru had more experience in the soap business than probably anyone but old man Procter himself, his advice was followed. But though we spent millions, we never seemed to make any gain on our main competitor. After several failures and disappointments, we began to realize that the problem was that our guru's information and advice was based solely on past experience. Since the whole industry, from the competition to customers' buying habits, was changing, his solutions were outdated and prevented us from coming up with something new.

If you try to solve *today's* problems with *yesterday's* answers, you'll be gone *tomorrow*.

The Danger of Knowing the Right Answer

Dr. James Fadiman, an author and a business consultant, taught me an exercise I often use in my seminars, which shows the dangers of thinking you always know the correct way to address a problem.

I give the participants a Crayola crayon and a piece of paper with the rules of a game. The game is called Nine Dots. In case you haven't played it, I have listed the rules below. (If you have played the game, don't think you know the answer—read on.)

The goal of the game is to join the nine dots using a maximum of four lines, *without taking your marker off the paper, without passing through any dot more than once, and without retracing any line.*

Many people who have struggled with this game know that the solution is to go outside the lines, or "out of the box"—which is where that expression comes from.

An answer to the problem looks like this.

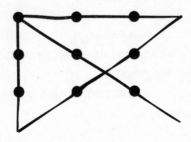

But here's the real problem. People who know that solution just do it. They put down their crayons and stop looking for any other possibilities. After the allotted time, I have someone show us their out-of-the-box solution.

Then I ask for any *other* possibilities. Silence generally follows.

I then show them two other possible solutions. One is to tear the wrapping off the crayon and draw one broad line through all the dots using the *length* of the crayon rather than the point. Fadiman, incidentally, told me he learned this from a schoolkid.

Another solution is to tear the paper vertically along the

lines of the dots and then connect the three in a straight line. And there's more. In his book *Conceptual Blockbusting*, James L. Adams has five other solutions to this problem![5]

The point of the exercise is that the people who "knew" the solution to this game didn't look any further. This attitude of thinking you know the right answer limits one's thinking and prevents new possibilities from being found.

One of my rules for innovation is: Don't stop at your first idea; always look beyond it for a second one.

NO EXPERIENCE NECESSARY

Some of the most successful leaders are people who, prior to taking over the top slot, had no experience in that field. How can this be? you might ask. How can someone who has no experience in a business be successful? Best-selling author and Harvard Business School professor John Kotter says that "outsiders have the intuitive ability to continually view problems in fresh ways and to identify ineffective practices and traditions."[6]

Gary Hamel writes, "More often than not, industries get reinvented by outsiders free from the prejudices of industry veterans."[7] Examples of these include Ted Turner and broadcast news (CNN), Anita Rodick and cosmetics (The Body Shop), Jeff Bezos and retailing (Amazon.com) and Pierre Omidyar and auctions (eBay). Louis Gerstner, who turned around IBM, came from the food business.

Lack of retail experience wasn't a problem for Home Depot's new president Bob Nardelli. Nardelli comes from GE, where in three decades he moved through a variety of very different types of businesses, from appliances to lighting to transportation systems. In his last job there, he headed GE Power Systems. Though he had no experience selling generators and heavy duty equipment to the energy industry, he increased revenues in what was thought to be a mature business from $6 billion to $15 billion in five years. "It's easy for me to come in and change things because I don't have the institutionalized point of view," says Nardelli.[8]

Fresh Ideas

When George Kirkland, the president of the Los Angeles Convention and Visitors Bureau, one of the largest in the country, was looking to hire a company to do their marketing plan, he didn't look for one with expertise in the convention and tourism field. He hired a consultant who had worked with giant packaged goods companies like Procter & Gamble. "I wanted to get some fresh ideas and I thought that my best chance of that was to link up with a premier consumer products team with no experience in our industry," Kirkland said.[9] He got what he was seeking, a revolutionary strategy that totally reinvented their business.

In 1987, Bill Wilkinson, along with his son, started Corporate Staffing Resources, a recruiting firm that now has sales of over $300 million. Wilkinson's background? Human resources? Head-hunting? Recruiting? Hardly. For twenty-eight years he worked in sales and management for Central Soya, a $1.5 billion international food and grain company.

Silicon Valley venture capitalist Robert Kagle plucked Meg Whitman from her job promoting Teletubbies at Hasbro Toys to head up eBay. Under her stewardship the Internet auction house has become a fantastic success. Her background prior to Hasbro was also hardly high tech. She was the CEO of Florists' Transworld Delivery (FTD).

Regarding this seemingly unconventional hire, Kagle said, "I was looking for a brand builder to help make eBay a household name. Understanding technology was not the central ingredient. Executives today are becoming to technology what McDonalds founder Ray Kroc was to fast foods in the early sixties. In those days an executive didn't have to know the chemistry of ground beef to deliver the hamburger people wanted. Today's Internet executives do not have to be computer geniuses but seasoned brand managers."[10]

Novel Ideas from Novices

If you really want to get some great new ideas or find out what's not working in your organization, talk to people with the least experience. Recent hires, especially in industries like retail, are often closer in age and interests to the customer and will therefore usually have better ideas and instincts about new products and services.

Beginners see obvious problems and opportunities that experts overlook. Several years ago a major jeans company was manufacturing most of its garments in the Southeast, then shipping them to the company's main distribution center on the West Coast, which was the site of its corporate headquarters. But a recent hire in the shipping department wanted to know, "Why are we shipping the jeans from the Southeast to the West when most of our markets are in the East?" That simple question from a junior employee saved the company several million dollars.

When John Calley was one of the nighttime clerks at NBC, he noticed that all the scenery for television shows was being sent down the warehouse elevator on one dolly and then transferred to another because the first dolly was too big for the second elevator. This changing of dollies took considerable time and labor.

Pointing this out in a memo to his supervisor, Calley suggested that the company build one dolly that would fit both elevators. "It was obvious that what they were doing was insane. But no one thought of it before. The change was made immediately and the savings amounted to several hundred thousand dollars,"[11] says Calley, who later became the CEO of United Artists.

Gorilla Talk

Another example of the wisdom of beginners occurred during the filming of the movie *Gorillas in the Mist*. Aside from Rwanda being on the verge of revolution and the difficulties of filming in the middle of a jungle, one of the biggest problems was the concern that since the gorillas might not follow instructions, dwarfs in gorilla suits would have to be used. Needless to say, no one wanted gorilla suits.

An emergency meeting to solve this problem was going nowhere when a young intern, working on her first film, asked, "What if you let the gorillas write the story?" Everyone laughed off her suggestion, but since nothing else was available, someone asked her what she meant. "What if you sent a really good cinematographer into the jungle with a ton of film to shoot the gorillas? Then write the story around what the gorillas did on film."[12] Taking her advice resulted in phenomenal footage. This young woman's idea not only saved the movie from being shelved but cut the cost of the film to half the original budget.

"This woman's inexperience enabled her to see opportunities where we saw only boundaries," said Mandalay Entertainment Chairman Peter Gruber. Gruber discovered the secret "was to find people who add new perspectives and create new conversations. You'll be surprised at what you discover."[13]

WIPE THE SLATE CLEAN

You don't have to be a beginner to think like one. At a Hewlett Packard plant in Roseville, California, they used the beginner's thinking technique for wiping the slate clean to redesign their new assembly line. Questioning every part of the operation from computer systems to cafeteria, they totally revamped the line. By approaching their work with fresh eyes, they cut raw material expense by 50 percent and went from a fifty- to a four-screw design for the computer terminal. Paperwork was reduced by 90 percent, and time spent on labor to build the terminals was cut by 75 percent.

One way to instill a beginner's mind-set in your operation is to do the same thing—*wipe the slate clean*. Restart your business. Start fresh. Imagine it is the first day on your job. What would you do differently? What would you stop doing? Challenge everything. Nothing is sacred.

Switching Jobs

Another way to develop a beginner's mind-set is to switch jobs. A major international chemical company discovered this inadvertently during a union walkout at one of their plants. To keep the plant running, they staffed it with people from many other departments, such as engineering and research. It took a week or so for these people, who had no experience running the factory, to get up to speed. In a relatively short while, not only were they running the plant efficiently, but they also cut costs, streamlined the production line, and increased productivity.

Perkin-Elmer, a manufacturer of analytical instruments and semiconductor equipment, brought in people who had no expertise in engineering to consult on an engineering problem. These "nonspecialists" cut the number of changes required to produce a product by 50 percent and manufacturing costs by as much as 55 percent! How? By simply questioning everything they didn't understand. Based on their findings, plans for a new bolt-in metal fan were scrapped in favor of a plastic one that easily snapped into place and was cheaper to boot.[14]

At a major ski resort we had managers spend two hours a week for twelve weeks in a department in which they had virtually no experience. The maintenance manager went to retail, the ski school director went to food service, and so on.

At the end of three months these "beginners" came up with questions that led to major innovations. Ticket lines were cut in half and the traffic flow in the retail and rental operations was totally altered and resulted in increased business and reduced waiting. One suggestion involving lift ticket sales resulted in a savings of over fifty thousand dollars. All this accomplished by beginners doing expert work.

The Value of Asking "Stupid" Questions

One of the reasons that switching jobs works so well is that when people work in the same area for a while they develop habits that quickly turn into routines and ultimately ruts. The result is an attachment to the routines and a resistance to challenging them and finding new ways of doing things. Why fix it if it ain't broke?

Neophytes with fresh eyes will often see things in an operation that others who have been on the job for years and have developed "experience blinders" don't see. They ask "stupid" questions that challenge old roles. Two of the best questions are, "How come you are doing that?" and "Why is this being done this way?" It is often this type of question that shakes things up, arouses people from their lethargy, and creates innovation.

At a plant that manufactured automobile tires, a member of the information technology staff asked why they were wrapping the tires in foil prior to shipping. The reason, he was told, was to prevent returns of whitewalls that were scuffed in shipping. "But only 3 percent of the tires are whitewalls," he replied.

It turned out that twenty years ago, when over 75 percent of tires were whitewalls, many that got dirty in shipping were being returned. At that point they decided to wrap the tires in an effort to significantly decrease returns. And it worked but was now completely outdated. All it took was a techie with no manufacturing experience to question the operation, which was then eliminated, and the company saved twenty-four million dollars. Go figure.

Through the Eyes of a Child

A bank president brought his twelve-year-old daughter into work one day, showed her around, and introduced her to all his colleagues. On their drive home he asked her if she liked the bank. Much to his surprise, she said, "No!"

"Why?" her shocked father asked.

"No one looked like they were having fun. No one was smiling," the young girl said.

He mentioned the incident at a companywide meeting and found out that it was exactly as his daughter had said. People weren't having any fun. They felt overly pressured: upper management was stifling innovation and there was too much micromanaging and too many meaningless meetings. This young girl's observation resulted in a revamping of the bank's culture.

Bring your kid into your work and try the same thing. Or bring your mother or father. Don't try to explain why you are doing things the way you are, just listen to them. I guarantee you will get some feedback and ideas that will open your eyes.

Seeing the Obvious

Back in 1988, Anthony Migliore, a college student, noticed an older man bagging groceries in a supermarket. Migliore later discovered that the man had been an IBM executive who retired and took this job to fight boredom. He then figured that in Florida, the land of retirees, there were probably loads of other individuals doing similar jobs and that there were probably many companies who would pay for their expertise.

He founded Seniorstaff, a temporary help agency, which has over two thousand employees, such as retired bankers filling in at local branches, former salespeople driving limos, and homemakers stuffing envelopes. Last year his business was up 400 percent from the previous year.

Beginner's Practice

Many of the greatest ideas and opportunities are right in front of our eyes. Yet experience has blinded us to them. We tend to seek the obscure rather than the obvious, the complex rather than the simple.

It's important to practice opening your mind and thinking like a beginner. Here's a game you can try. Pick up any object and pretend you have never seen it before. I held up a coffee cup in a workshop, saying to the group, "Pretend you are a Martian and have never seen this object before. And write down as many uses as you can."

Some of the answers: a cookie mold, a paperweight, a rolling pin, a hat, a musical instrument, and a listening device.

➠ KEEP IN MIND
- ➠ Wipe the slate clean.
- ➠ Be curious, question everything.
- ➠ Listen down—the most novel ideas often come from novices.
- ➠ Bring your child to work.

[1] Wind Bell Green Gulch Zen Center Bulletin, Fall 1998.
[2] *Fortune*, 24 February 1992, p. 79.
[3] *Fortune*, 30 April 2001, p. 77.
[4] *Fortune*, 12 June 2000, p. 104.
[5] James L. Adams, *Conceptual Blockbusting* (Cambridge: Perseus Books, 1986).
[6] *Fortune*, 24 February 1992, p. 79.
[7] *Fortune*, 12 June 2000, p. 104.
[8] *Fortune*, 19 March 2001, p. 88.
[9] Personal communication, 6 July 2000.
[10] *New York Times*, 10 May 1999, p. C1.
[11] *The New Yorker*, 21 March 1994, p. 80.
[12] *Fast Company*, June/July 1998, p. 90.
[13] Ibid.
[14] *Business Week*, December 1989, p. 107.

CHAPTER 11

Challenge Your Assumptions

THE FARMER'S DILEMMA

Take a few minutes to solve this problem.

A farmer is taking a duck, a fox, and some corn seed to the market when he comes to a deep, fast-moving creek. Though he has a rowboat, it is small and fits only one piece of cargo at a time. The fox can't swim and the stream is moving too fast for the duck.

The farmer knows that if he takes the corn seed first and leaves the duck and the fox alone, the fox will eat the duck. But if he takes the fox across, the duck will eat the corn seed. If he takes the duck first, and then the fox, the fox will eat the duck when he goes back for the corn seed.

So he sits there scratching his head.

Have you got any advice for the farmer?

If you're scratching your head like the farmer, you're probably making the same assumption that he did, which prevented him from solving the problem: *that he had to return back across the lake with an empty boat.*

Challenging that assumption makes the solution quite obvious. First the farmer takes the duck across and returns empty. He then takes the corn seed to the other side. He leaves the corn seed but puts the duck back in the boat and returns, whereupon he leaves the duck and takes the fox across. He then leaves the fox with the corn seed and goes back for the duck.

OLD TRUTHS

Like the farmer, many of us fail to solve problems and miss out on opportunities or alternate possibilities because of the unexamined assumptions that we make. It's important to realize that the assumptions we make about a situation, people, and ourselves strongly influence the decisions we make and the actions we take. If, for instance, you assume someone isn't going to buy into your idea, you'll give up before you start and either not try very hard or not try at all. Both reactions will ensure that your assumption becomes self-fulfilling and you'll miss out on an opportunity.

Sometimes our assumptions are valid. Often they were true at one time. But since everything is changing, from technology, to the customer, to the competition, assumptions that were true in the past are often outdated. As a result, unchecked assumptions can cause you to spend a lot of time, energy, and resources working on something that is no longer valid.

FINDING NEW OPPORTUNITIES BY CHALLENGING OLD ASSUMPTIONS

Some of the most successful businesses were developed and later revolutionized by people who challenged old assumptions. In the freight shipping business, for instance, the assumption was always that the fastest way for a package to get from one place to another was to ship it directly to its destination. It seemed to make sense, so that's the way all the freight companies did it. Then Fred Smith came along and challenged that assumption with a hub-and-spoke model that revolutionized the freight business. His idea was to ship all packages, regardless of their shipping point or destination, to a central hub in Memphis, Tennessee. From there they would be rerouted to their destination. Sounds crazy, right? Well, that's what everyone thought, including his teacher at Yale, who gave him a C for the paper that proposed that idea. But by challenging the old thinking, Fred Smith created Federal Express.

The old assumption in broadcasting was that the news was aired once an hour for five minutes, at the top of the hour. Along came master convention challenger Ted Turner with CNN, which aired the news all the time. Microsoft's Bill Gates, Domino's Tom Monaghan, Sam Walton, and hundreds of other pioneers became incredibly successful by challenging the basic assumptions of their respective industries.

The same is true in sports. Dick Fosbury won a gold medal, set a world record, and changed the high jump event forever by challenging the assumption that you had to jump feet first.

Coach Bill Walsh won five Super Bowls as coach of the San Francisco 49ers by challenging the most basic rule of offensive football: that your passing attack could only be successful if you first established a running game. Walsh's West Coast offense, which is now being used on all coasts, revolutionized offensive football by doing the opposite. He used the pass to set up the run.

The old assumption in tennis was you made one-handed strokes. Then along came Chris Evert and Jimmy Connors with their two-handed strokes that changed the way most people play today.

Mixing Doing Well with Doing Good

Have you ever applied for a bank loan or mortgage? They want to know everything—your past, your future, your total financial and credit history. And if one thing doesn't check out—poof! You're history.

Then there's Muhammed Yunus, the founder of the Grameen Bank, headquartered in Dhaka, Bangladesh. Yunus's business premise, which has become a model for institutions in over fifty countries, challenged the basic assumptions of most financial institutions regarding loans. The Grameen Bank provides credit, not for the countries' richest people, but for the poorest.

Obviously with this type of customer Yunus doesn't try for the jumbo loans that all banks crave. His loans are sometimes as small as thirty dollars. And he doesn't ask for collateral. He does, however, require that the borrowers organize into small groups and guarantee each other's loans. And over 90 percent of his loans go to women.

Crazy, you say? Like a fox. Not only is Yunus a pioneer in fighting poverty, but his results from this micro-lending strategy have been spectacular. The Grameen Bank now has nearly 1,100 branches and has made more than two million loans worth over two billion dollars. Yeah, but what about defaults? you ask. Would you believe 2 percent?

"I am a businessman," Yunus says. "But it's business with a twist. I practice business with a social objective. We look for market solutions to social problems."[1]

Full Court

The assumption of many people getting a divorce is that they and their soon-to-be ex-spouse are opponents. So, they often hire a shark lawyer and go for the kill. They adopt an adversarial approach pitting one mate/lawyer team against the other.

Gary Friedman, a former successful trial lawyer, revolutionized divorce proceedings by challenging this assumption. He wondered why both parties couldn't be represented by one attorney in a more congenial atmosphere of cooperation and goodwill. He knew this approach would also save oodles of money.

People thought he was out of his mind. Just like they did with Fred Smith, Ted Turner, and pioneers as far back as Christopher Columbus who challenged old assumptions. Cooperation in a divorce case—fuhgeddaboudit! One lawyer for both people—no way!

Acting on this new premise, Friedman created a mediation practice for divorce proceedings in Mill Valley, California. That practice has grown tremendously, and Friedman now has an international reputation conducting mediation-training programs for lawyers and judges at both Stanford and Harvard law schools and throughout Europe. He has also worked with megacorporations in their merger negotiations.

Rounding Up Sacred Cows

Challenging assumptions isn't the purview of the great or near great. It doesn't have to involve creating rule-breaking new industries or businesses. Questioning your beliefs and assumptions is an important habit that can result in solving problems, spotting opportunities, and saving time, money, and energy in any area of your life.

Outdated assumptions create sacred cows such as all those policies, procedures, practices, systems, and strategies that once worked but have become obsolete and now waste time, cost money, and prevent new possibilities.

To put these sacred cows out to pasture, I often have companies go on sacred-cow hunts. It's a simple, yet incredibly effective practice that starts with a team or an individual challenging the assumption that underlies a policy or practice, by merely asking the question, "Why are we doing this?" The results from these hunts have been nothing short of amazing.

At a sacred-cow hunt at a deodorant manufacturing plant, one worker questioned why the bottles were individually boxed and then put in cartons with thick cardboard fillers. "We don't want the bottles to break in shipping" was the response. That reasoning was great when the bottles were made of glass, but two years prior they had switched to plastic bottles but had not stopped to rethink the packaging. Eliminating this practice saved the company $8 million.

The $24 million savings by the automobile tire manufacturing company (discussed in the previous chapter) that discovered they no longer had to wrap the tires was also a result of a sacred-cow hunt.

Sacred cows create waste at all levels. A group of sacred-cow hunters at a major Texas hospital found that the patient admittance kit included a male urinal, yet two thirds of their patients were women. Eliminating it saved them $5 thousand a year. The kit also included a bedpan that they discovered no one used. Eliminating that saved them $7,500.

MAKE THE INVISIBLE VISIBLE

Prior to making any decision, solving any problem, or developing any new strategy, it's important to determine the underlying assumptions you have about the situation.

An example of this became apparent at a conference with top managers at Genrad, a $500 million multinational electronic testing and measurement manufacturer. The purpose of the meeting was to develop a bold new vision and strategy for the company—in effect, to reinvent the organization. Prior to the work session, I had the group list the assumptions they had about the business. These are just a few of the entries that came from the group:

- We are a testing company.
- We are a software-driven company.
- We manufacture and sell only our own products.
- We have large plants and inventories.
- All of our products operate on a 60 percent margin and we have no low-cost products.
- Our customers are the automobile industry.
- We are *one* company.
- All the software engineers work directly for us.
- We have a large workforce.
- We can never really be a big company.

Reviewing the list helped the group realize how these assumptions were limiting their thinking and preventing any changes. Challenging each of them to determine the validity of each assumption enabled them to be much more innovative and expansive during the vision and strategy sessions.

DON'T JUDGE A BOOK

Another area where we often limit our possibilities involves the assumptions we make about people. We often jump to conclusions about someone because of what they do, how they look, what school they went to, where they come from, as well as from their beliefs and backgrounds.

You might assume that techies or accountants or engineers are boring. That promoters are full of hype and no substance and that lawyers are money hungry and heartless. These assumptions will dictate your attitude toward these individuals as well as how you communicate with them. You might lose out on a great idea by automatically writing off a suggestion from your secretary because you assume she isn't educated enough to have a good idea.

Some of the best ideas come from places and people you least expect. The reason you don't expect good things to come from them is because you assume that they are too young, too old, too uneducated, too overeducated, too freaky, or too _____ (you fill in the blank), to contribute anything worthwhile or meaningful.

Out-of-the-Box Funerals

Can you imagine a more staid, solemn, tradition-bound group than funeral directors? That was my assumption when I spoke at the International Cemetery and Funeral Association's annual meeting.

Facing many changes and new challenges in their industry, these funeral directors proved to be exactly the opposite. Pardon the pun, but many related examples of funerals that were literally "out of the box."

One told a story about a service that was particularly morose when suddenly one mourner yelled, "Hey, what would Joe want if he were here now?"

"He'd probably order out for Chinese food," another chimed in, and the group broke into laughter. Someone then ordered take-out for the group. Thirty minutes later, chopsticks in hand, eating pot stickers and princess shrimp, they spent the rest of the culinary send-off telling stories about Joe.

"It was one of the warmest, most heartfelt services I ever presided over," the director said.

And how about a funeral that was actually a *hayride* for the deceased? "That's how we met," his wife had explained. It had become their annual tradition. "This is how I want to remember him; it brings back such sweet memories."

Another told of a funeral that featured a slide show and pictures showing the deceased at all ages in her life.

These funeral directors had flipped the rules: Instead of insisting that funerals be about mourning a death, they let them be celebrations of a life.

My experiences with these tradition-busting funeral directors as well as many others taught me to check my assumptions at the door about any individual or group.

Don't Dismiss Anyone's Ideas

Dismissing people's suggestions because of their education or background can be costly and cause you to miss out on numerous opportunities.

Maria Gonzales, who spent over twenty years in the laundry department at Hillcrest Baptist Hospital, designed a new hospital gown and the hospital has sold more than five hundred thousand of them.

Jeremy Johnson, who dropped out of college to be a ski bum, came up with an idea to sell hot drinks from his snowmobile to people who were cold while waiting on the lift line. When the idea was fully developed, it earned profits of more than $2 million for the ski resort.

If you're using college grades to determine a person's value, how about the fact that over 50 percent of CEOs of major corporations had C or C- averages in college. And that 65 percent of U.S. senators and 75 percent of all U.S. presidents came from the bottom half of their class. How about all those incredibly successful entrepreneurs who never even graduated college, such as Bill Gates and Steve Jobs? Not to mention those who never made it to college or who didn't graduate from high school, such as Jim Clark, who founded Silicon Graphics and Netscape.

Don't Be a Mind Reader

Several years ago there were many books and programs focusing on learning to read body language in order to improve communications or manipulate someone into buying something they didn't need. As a result we often make assumptions about what someone is feeling or thinking based on their body language.

Folded arms, for instance, are supposed to indicate that the person is closed and usually angry. A clenched jaw means they are tense. The person who peeks at his watch or yawns during a presentation is bored. A person scratching their head doesn't believe you. And so on.

We then act on that assumption. We talk louder and faster to get the watch peeker's attention. We overexplain to the head scratcher to convince him of our point. But as with any assumption you make, it may or may not be true. The watch peeker may have a sick spouse at home and is waiting to hear from the doctor. Or maybe he got a new watch and likes to look at it. The person yawning possibly didn't get any sleep the night before. And maybe the head scratcher has dandruff.

But because we act on our assumptions, they become self-fulfilling. The watch peeker is now turned off because you are talking too fast and too loud. And because you seem to be overselling your point, the head scratcher is now really starting to doubt what you are saying.

People are complex. A body signal from one person may mean something totally different when done by another. So don't make assumptions based on what you think people are feeling or thinking. Jumping to conclusions may cause them to jump right back at you.

))))➤ KEEP IN MIND

➡ Check assumptions before making decisions.
➡ Round up sacred cows and put them out to pasture.
➡ Don't use yesterday's thinking in today's game.

CHAPTER 12

Flip the Rules

The term "out of the box" has become so common and overused that "out of the box" now has become "in the box." But what does all this talk about a box really mean? What is the "box" anyway? And how do you get out of it?

THE 180-DEGREE FLIP

One way to get out of the box or break it down is to take a problem, assumption, or strategy and flip it 180 degrees. Michael Dell did just that in the computer industry. Challenging the old industry practice of stockpiling inventory, one of the biggest costs for a computer maker, Dell did just the opposite. Dell Computer has no inventory and only manufactures those PCs for which they receive orders. This twist on the old thinking not only eliminates the costs of keeping a huge inventory but enables Dell to customize each computer for the individual customer. This innovative breakthrough has been so effective that it is being copied by computer giants such as IBM and Compaq as well as automobile manufacturers such as Ford and GM.

Sam Walton did the same thing in retail. The old rules for success in retail were location, location, location. You had to have a high-traffic, center-of-the-mall or downtown location to be successful. Walton gave that rule a twist and opened Wal-Mart's first giant warehouse store in the booming metropolis of Rogers, Arkansas. Instead of opening in *big* markets, he started in *small*, rural ones. Crowds came and Wal-Mart is now the *Big* Daddy of retail. One of Mr. Sam's most important rules of success was that if everyone in your industry is doing it one way, do it exactly the opposite.

The same thing happened in the fast-food industry. At a time when the competition was trying every trick, gimmick, and incentive to get *you* into *their* store, Domino's Pizza founder Tom Monaghan flipped that thinking. He recognized that convenience was becoming increasingly important for two-paycheck, time-starved families. So instead of trying to get *them* into *his* store, he brought *his* store to *them*. Banana Republic is doing the same thing. They are holding fashion shows, and displaying and selling their merchandise, in company offices. And many online brokers are flipping the established practice and moving from clicks to bricks to offer clients personal service. E*Trade has four-hundred-square-foot E*Trade zones inside super Target stores. DLJDirect is opening offices in New York, Chicago, Atlanta, Dallas, and Silicon Valley.[1]

This type of thinking isn't restricted to the giants. When chef Peter Brown started Foursquare Catering in San Francisco, he was having trouble getting business. Brown's strategy was to invite prospective clients for lunch to sample his specialties. But no one came. The problem was that all of his competitors were using the same strategy. And many people didn't want to take time out of their busy day to come over to his place.

In a version of "If you can't make Mohammed come to the mountain, bring the mountain to Mohammed," he decided to give his strategy a twist. Rather than trying to get clients to come to *his* place, he offered to set up a special lunch at their office. The response was overwhelming (who doesn't want a free lunch?). Giving his strategy a flip enabled Brown to land some of the biggest clients in the Bay Area and launch a very successful business.

CUTTING CORNERS

Ray Evernham, with driver Jeff Gordon, used this flip-of-the-rules strategy in NASCAR racing to win the Winston Cup Championship several times. Evernham says, "If conventional wisdom says the corner is the best place to pass, we practice passing on the other end of the track, because nobody is expecting to get passed there."[2]

The following are some examples of how to use that 180-degree flip to solve old problems and create new possibilities.

Hitting the Jackpot

It's always exciting to think about how much you might win if you hit the lottery. As a business, however, the lottery isn't doing as well as it once did. Its growth has actually been pretty flat for the last couple of years. One of the biggest problems is that young people aren't playing the lottery.

In an effort to make the lottery more appealing for the twenty-something generation, I had the heads of state lotteries in one of my groups review the basic components of the game. Here's what they listed:

a. One big prize. Sure, it's mouthwateringly attractive, but there's still only one of them.

b. Delayed gratification. You have to wait to hear if you won.

c. Luck. There's no skill at all in buying a ticket.

d. Passive. There's no active involvement.

It immediately became obvious why the lottery wasn't attractive to a younger generation that had grown up playing dynamic video games. I then had them give each element a 180-degree flip. The result was a game that would have much more appeal for younger people and is now being considered in several states.

a. Many prizes.

b. Instant gratification—you would know immediately if you won.

c. Active and skill oriented.

d. Visually exciting and fun to play.

You can use this same technique with your "game." Start by listing the basic components, elements, or rules of your job or business. Then give each a flip. Odds are this little exercise will open up new possibilities.

CONQUERING SABOTAGE THINKING

When developing a plan with a client, I flip the rules and start out by thinking not what we have to do to succeed, but rather what we might inadvertantly do to sabotage the program. Being aware of our own tendency toward sabotage thinking helps us avoid being victimized by it.

A group working on a new product presentation for a prospective client made out the following list of ways they could ensure their presentation would fail:

- Do an inadequate job of understanding the client's business.
- Keep your credentials and past successes a secret.

- Show rough drawings rather than a customized prototype.
- Rave about the product but not the benefits to the client.
- Don't research who will be attending the meeting.
- Arrive at the last minute, stressed from racing in traffic.
- Use lots of buzzwords and industry jargon.
- Don't scope out the conference room in advance.
- Don't rehearse the presentation, wing it.
- Assume they will have the right equipment for our presentation.
- Don't be enthusiastic, be dull and talk down to them.

Making up a sabotage list is fun and helps to identify and anticipate some of the unconscious ways that we undermine our own efforts. Once these have been identified, it is easy to flip these potential sabotages around to successes.

More to Less

Half of the beds in a major metropolitan hospital were empty. The hospital tried everything from new alliances to new marketing approaches to running over people in the streets in order to fill the beds. Nothing worked.

Flipping the old thinking enabled them to uncover a new solution. Realizing that hospitals, run by insurance companies, were no longer in the bed business, but in the keep-you-*out*-of-bed business, I asked them, "Instead of trying to *fill* beds, why don't we think about emptying them?" The solution that eventually emerged was to sell the beds and create a wellness wing with a sports medicine clinic, a health club, educational programs, a dietary facility, and a pharmacy.

One of the exercises we did that helped us make this decision was to list the benefits of shifting the hospital wing to a wellness center.

Hospital	Wellness Center
Market: sick people	Larger market: healthy people
Short-term intervention	Ongoing relationships
Large facilities	Small
Expensive capital equipment	Inexpensive equipment
High overhead—expensive staff	Low overhead—outsource trainers, MDs, nurses, legal
Single transaction	Repeat business, support groups
Big administration	Small administration
Restricted revenue/insurance	No income restriction/other possible sources of income: facelifts, transplants (non-insurance-based), educational programs, trips, events
Sterile, depressing environment	High-energy, fun environment
Drugs, healing sick	Educating on healthy lifestyle
Trend: home care, less time in hospital	Trend: more people physically active, interested in health and fitness
Stringent regulations	Less-stringent regulations

Flipping the old thinking from that of curing sick people to one of preventing people from getting sick created a much healthier hospital. Revenue from the wellness wing was three times what they would have realized by filling the beds.

Trading New for Old

Directors of museum stores felt stymied in their efforts to bring more *new* customers *into* the store. Flipping this strategy, I had them focus on how to get more *old* customers—in other words, how to encourage repeat business. Ideas that emerged included a membership organization offering special incentives such as discounts, monthly events with artists, and an expanded product line.

Then, instead of getting people *into* the store, we explored the idea of bringing the store to them. This 180-degree change opened up many new possibilities, including mail-order catalogues, Web sites, participation in local craft fairs and gift shows, mall stores, and displays in corporate head-quarters. The result was an average revenue increase in a nine-month pilot program of 36 percent.

From Top to Bottom

We're not talking rocket science. This strategy is simple: Take a problem and give it a twist, and you will often spot a new opportunity. The president of a large children's wear manufacturer was wrestling with how to get her *top* people more involved. Flipping this around, she began thinking about how to get her *bottom* people more involved. With this new focus, she began seeking ways to empower her employees, and changed her whole management style.

Her workers were soon more motivated and involved and began contributing ideas that streamlined the operation, cut costs, and improved customer service. In fact, one of the ideas she received from a production line worker cut the time it took from receiving an order to delivering it by over 30 percent.

From Recruiting to Retaining

A problem for most companies these days is how to recruit good people. This is especially true in minimum-wage and entry-level jobs in fast-food franchises, supermarkets, and retail. As a result of this type of environment, the turnover rate for one fast-food franchisee, who owned five stores, was almost 90 percent, and the annual expense for recruiting and training new employees was in excess of $75,000. "Gotta get some good people," he told me. "I've been trying everything, including going to the local high schools and community colleges. But most of these kids last a few weeks and then off they go to something else."

He then decided to flip the rules from how to *get* good people to how to *keep* them. He began focusing on how to make his restaurants more enjoyable places to work. Staff parties were thrown every month when they made a profit, and people were rewarded when they did something special.

This new campaign immediately motivated people. Yet his turnover rate was still fairly high when he came up with the barn-burner idea that resulted from a conversation he had with one of his assistant managers. Tapping into young people's hopes and dreams, he told his people that if they worked for him for two years, he would pay their way through college. No, not to Yale or some other pricey private college, but to the local community or business college. It worked. In two years his turnover rate went from 90 percent to less than 8 percent. And his cost of recruiting and training was cut to under $5,000. Furthermore, he now owns eleven fast-food restaurants, and four of them are being managed by people from this program.

From Shotgun to Laser

When Colin Chen became the vice president of worldwide sales and marketing for Hewlett Packard's component group, sales were $500 million and growing glacially. The strategy at the time was to try and sell as many products as possible to as many clients as possible. Chen flipped the rules from essentially a shotgun to a laser strategy by initiating a "big win" approach that focused only on major accounts. As a result, the company went from ten thousand accounts of all sizes to five hundred major ones. Today the spin-off company, Agilent, under Chen's leadership, has only three hundred accounts and is doing $3 billion in sales. Salespeople that were previously doing $1–2 million a year are now averaging revenues of $16–18 million a year.

From Cost Center to Profit Center

City and state governments are constantly seeking ways to decrease their budgets in order to please their constituencies. The result is that organizations like fire departments are constantly struggling to cut costs. Many firefighters are burning out trying to do more with less and wearing many hats and working longer shifts.

At a conference of fire chiefs, I suggested flipping the thinking from being an income drain to becoming an income generator. This shift involved finding new sources of revenues, such as providing emergency medical aid, running ambulance services for hospitals, cleaning up disaster sites, and being the first to respond at other emergency situations.

A great model for this type of unconventional thinking is Kansas City's Overland Park Fire Department, which has become a profit center rather than a cost center for the city. In addition to offering some of the above-mentioned services, this entrepreneurial fire company rents out their facility for training programs to telecommunications companies such as Sprint as well as to military and industrial organizations, community colleges, and other fire departments. They even rent out their multipurpose room for corporate stockholder meetings. Rather than taking money from the city, this entrepreneurial outfit generates more than a quarter of a million dollars for the city. Check out their Web site (www.opfd.com) if you want to see some examples of "nonprofit" potential.

Raise Your Prices, Don't Lower Them

These days one manufacturer's products are perceived by the customer as pretty much the same as the rest of the competition. The result is that consumers are increasingly shopping for the best deal. Companies are therefore scrambling to do anything they can to cut costs and prices. But price cutting is ultimately a losing game, since someone, somewhere, is always willing to sell cheaper, even to the point of losing money, in order to make inroads with the customer.

My approach is to increase rather than decrease prices. The focus then becomes finding ways to differentiate your product or service and add value so that you are no longer competing with the price cutters.

Don't Start at the Beginning

Whether it is a book or a proposal, many people have difficulty starting a writing project. That first step seems like an insurmountable hurdle. The first line seems impossible to get right.

One way to get yourself going is to begin at the end or the middle. I have started out writing my last three books with those chapters that I am most excited and clear about. I will often begin writing a chapter, not necessarily at what I think should be the beginning, but with a great story or example that I enjoy relating and that clearly illustrates the point I want to make. Once started, momentum builds and the rest becomes much easier, whether you have to go forward or backward or both.

From We to You

Actually the whole marketplace has undergone a 180-degree turn. In the past the belief was that the customer buys what we make. Now it is: We make what people want, how they want it, and sell it to them where they want. In other words, we have gone from a manufacturing-driven culture to a customer-driven one.

This flip in perspective is also happening in the larger context. "Before, when we talked about macroeconomics, we started by looking at the local markets, financial systems, and the international economy," says Jacob Frenkel, a University of Chicago–trained economist and governor of Israel's Central Bank. "Now we reverse the perspective. Let's not ask what markets we should export to *after* deciding what to produce, rather first study the global framework within which we operate and *then* decide what to produce."[3]

Flipping

In school we learn and are rewarded for being rational, logical, linear thinkers. But innovation is often the opposite. Out-of-the-box thinking is usually nonlinear, counterintuitive, and seemingly illogical. You'll be amazed at the different perspective you get from these new angles, and the myriad of new possibilities, opportunities, and solutions that will emerge.

➡ **KEEP IN MIND**

➡ Give your thinking a 180-degree flip.

➡ If everyone is doing it one way, consider the opposite.

➡ Start at the top, not the bottom; the back, not the front; the end, not the beginning.

[1] *USA Today*, 1 November 2000, p. B1.

[2] *Fast Company*, October 1998, p. 176.

[3] Thomas Friedman, *The Lexus and the Olive Tree* (New York: Anchor Books, 2000), p. 10.

CHAPTER 13

Strange Combinations

ONE PLUS ONE EQUALS THREE

Not so long ago the rule was to find a niche and exploit it. Focus exclusively on one product, service, or market. A bookstore sold books. You want coffee and a place to sit and read, go to a coffee shop or diner. Supermarkets sold food, period. The telephone company sold phone service.

Now the game has changed. Bookstores sell coffee; food markets sell tires; health clubs have Internet hookups; telephone companies sell television programming; banks sell sandwiches, drugs, stocks, insurance, and now even want to sell you a house. Odd combinations of products and services have become increasingly common in a marketplace focused on one-stop shopping and owning the customer.

"Innovation often results when ideas or things are brought together in a way that never happened before, and when such juxtaposition occurs, the result is greater than the sum of the parts. One and one make three," writes James Burke in a *Time* magazine feature on inventions. "In the late nineteenth century, Wilhelm Maybach, an engineer for Daimler, put together the newly invented perfume sprayer with the newly discovered gasoline and comes up with the carburetor. In 1823, Scottish chemist Charles Macintosh, working with a throwaway coal tar by-product called Napthat (used to clean dying vats), stumbles across the fact that it will liquefy rubber. So he spreads the rubber between layers of cloth and invents the raincoat."[1]

One way to generate ideas that will give you an edge in a hybrid marketplace is to look far outside of your "box" to combine products, services, or markets that haven't previously been combined. Jacob Rabinow, who has received a Lifetime Achievement Award for invention from the Lemelson-MIT Awards program, says that: "The inventor has to remember things that seemingly have nothing to do with each other and then put them together in a way that is totally surprising."[2] This type of out-of-your-niche thinking will enable you to redefine your business, broaden its scope, and appeal to a wider customer base.

Selling coffee and food changed the nature of retail bookstores. Now they are a place not just to buy books and magazines, but for people to meet, study, and hang out. The result is an increase in store traffic and revenues.

The Sports Barber

Don't let yesterday's definition of your business determine how you do business today. Learn as much as you can about your clientele: their habits, interests, concerns, lifestyles, goals, and dreams. Then look to combine some offerings that, though diverse in nature, will appeal to your customer.

After taking an intensive course in barber school, Hannah Watkins, a retired nurse, recently opened a barbershop in a small town in northern California. Since there were two other established barbers in the area, she wanted to do something different. To get a better handle on her customers, she offered a wide array of magazines and newspapers for them to read while they were waiting in the chair. Sports magazines were the most popular. Hannah's customers loved to talk about sports, for which she shares a similar passion.

Copying popular sports bars, she put in a large-screen TV and tunes it to a ball game or sports show, or she plays videos of historic sporting events. And every week she posts trivia questions. The result is a sports barbershop that has definitely been a home run.

Gangster Cars and Soccer Moms

Remember the long-hooded gangster cars of the 1930s that used to roar around Chicago in *The Untouchables* TV series (if you are old enough) and in hundreds of movies? Can you imagine anything more different from that car than the minivans that soccer moms drive to cart around the kids? Well, Chrysler combined elements of these two models and introduced an eccentric design called the PT Cruiser. This hybrid has been such a hot seller that dealers across the country have monthlong waiting lists.

Internet Portals and Sweepstakes

Jonas Steinman, a health care investor at Chase Partners, and Bill Daugherty, a vice president at the National Basketball Association, were chatting over lunch one day about how all search engines looked alike. Musing about what it would take to build a different kind of portal, Daugherty happened to mention that the most successful promotion he had ever seen was McDonald's Monopoly Sweepstakes, in which the company gave away up to $1 million.

Bingo! Out of this conversation was born iWon.com, the first portal to offer Internet users what all other search engines don't have—a true alternative to Yahoo. Steinman and Daugherty combined two proven concepts, an Internet portal and a sweepstakes. IWon gives away about $27 million in prize money a year, which actually only costs them about $17 million because they pay out the big winner over time.[3] That's significantly less than the advertising revenues they generate.

The result of this unusual combination is that iWon, in less than a year after its launch, has grown so fast that it has become the number two portal after Yahoo.

Lighting a Dark, Wet Way

When you're out on a dark, stormy night, your umbrella helps keep you dry. But it's still dark and difficult to see. Many people go out in these conditions with both a flashlight and an umbrella. The Totes Isotoner Corporation, which sells about one third of the 35 million umbrellas purchased annually in the United States, solved this dilemma by creating a product that lights your way as well as keeps you dry. It's an umbrella with a flashlight in the handle and is called the Nightlighter 2000.

The Nightlighter 2000 was designed for a forty-two-year-old woman, Totes's average customer. It's small enough to fit into a purse and weighs only ten ounces when loaded with two AA batteries. The light is angled so the beam illuminates a walkway or the keyhole of a car.

The product came about when the company began exploring ways of making the handle more than just something you hang on to. Some of the other ideas: a compartment for keys, an AM/FM radio, and even a barometer so that the umbrella could tell you when it's likely to rain.

The Classified Game

I developed a game for people: to practice making odd combinations by distributing three pages from different parts of a classified phone book. The instructions are to select one business randomly from each page and combine each into a megabusiness. The goal is to spawn the most outrageous ideas.

Here are a few examples of "businesses" that have been generated by playing this game:

One group combined pet care, a dating service, and church and came up with a religious dating service for dogs.

Another combined a limo service, massage parlor, and clothing store. The result was a ride in a stretch limo to the clothing store while receiving a massage along the way.

Another combined mattresses, mausoleums, and a meat and sausage distributor and created a "business" that sold you a mattress with your mausoleum so that you could rest comfortably for eternity. And while your monument was being built, they would store you in a meat locker.

Still another creation was combining concrete contractors, garage door openers, and rug dealers to come up with Oriental-rug–patterned driveways and garage doors.

The goal of the game is not to be concerned with realistic ideas but to stretch your imagination and have some fun. Once you've opened your mind to this type of thinking, you can make the goal more realistic by listing your customers' diverse needs or habits. Then see if you can put them together. The clientele of one restaurant, who were mostly seniors, listed eating, schmoozing, and gambling as their favorite pastimes. The owner put these together, offering poker and bridge afternoons combined with lunch, and eventually bus trips to a casino that included meals along the way.

Upscale Discounting

In retail there are stores that cater to every segment of the market from the superrich to the coupon cutters and discount hunters. Catering to the upscale market, Neiman Marcus and Saks Fifth Avenue are at one end, with retailers like JCPenney, Kmart, and Wal-Mart at the other. But Target created a new strategy that spans the gamut. It's called upscale discounting. The message in their advertising says it all: "Looks like Barney's, priced like Kmart."

Called "Tarzhay" by the cognoscenti, Target has become the third-largest discounter by making it hip to shop there. Celebs are often snapped in Target gear, and the latest works of "in" designer Michael Graves are sold exclusively in their stores.

"Everybody now considers it cool to save money. On the other hand, is it cool to save money at Kmart or Wal-Mart? I don't think so," says New York retailing consultant Howard Dadivowitz. "You walk into Wal-Mart and there are these big boxes of corn flakes. How ugly. How totally uncool. Going to Target is a cool experience."[4]

Target combines discount prices with upmarket styling. *Fortune* magazine writer Shelly Branch wrote about how she had ordered a cocktail at the posh Four Seasons bar in New York City. "It arrived in a chic vessel: a tall, curvaceous martini glass with a zigzag stem."[5] She was so impressed that she thought that all sixteen-dollar drinks should be served like this. It was startling for her, a few days later, to see that very same glass featured in a Target ad for $3.69.

Target's motto is to price like a discounter but not to think like one. Combining these two opposite ends of the scale has enabled Target to compete with Kmart and JCPenney as well as with more upscale specialty chains such as Crate & Barrel and Banana Republic.

Mass Customizing

In most cases, mass marketing means exactly what it says— offer a few basic styles and sell them as cheaply as possible. No variations allowed. It's the approach Henry Ford took with his mass-produced Model T when he said that you could have any color you want as long as it was black.

Then there is the opposite approach, which involves buying more-expensive products and services that can be customized for your needs and tastes.

Up until a few years ago, computers were sold this way. If you wanted to save money, you could buy the inexpensive mass-market model. But as far as customizing it to meet your needs, their approach was you could get any color as long as it was black. If you wanted bells and whistles, you paid dearly for them. All that changed when Michael Dell came along with the concept of mass customizing. One of the most successful and profitable computer manufacturers, Dell Computers are very competitively priced. But each Dell computer is customized to your individual wants, needs, and specs.

This concept of mass customizing, which combines the two opposite ends of the scale, has become the model for manufacturers in just about every industry—from Dell's computer competitors to automobiles.

Home builders have also learned from Dell's model. The major builders used to mass-produce homes using the Levittown model. They were inexpensive and well built, but customization was limited to choosing between one of three standard models. That was it, except for a limited choice in the color of the carpet and tile. Custom homes were at the other end of the scale, specifically designed for your needs and tastes and very pricey.

Taking a page from Dell, the big mass builders still offer reasonably priced, well-built, mass-produced houses in several standard models, but now they also offer all kinds of options. You can pick the colors you want, change the elevations, the type of doors, stairs, windows, floor materials, and landscaping. You can have a room rewired for an office or add a fireplace. Sure, you're still in a big mass community, but each house is customized to fit the individual needs and tastes of the owner.

Combining Opposites

Here's an exercise to practice combining opposites. Take a moment and think about one aspect of your business. Then consider what the polar opposite is and see what you come up with. One garment manufacturer who did this exercise came up with loose tights and long shorts. The loose tights resulted in a line of comfortable exercise workout clothes. And long shorts have become a major fad with kids today, including those "kids" playing in the National Basketball Association.

To overcome creative blocks, poet Thomas Lynch, the author of *Bodies in Motion and at Rest*, uses the following exercise.

Combine one inanimate object in the house with something live outside. Or something you read in the newspaper with something you have heard on the radio.

There are unlimited opportunities for combinations just waiting to be tapped. The only limit is your thinking.

➟ **KEEP IN MIND**
- ➟ Combine unrelated concepts, products, and services.
- ➟ Mix opposites: old and new, short and long, high and low priced, mass and custom.
- ➟ Niches lead to ruts.

[1] *Time*, 4 December 2000, p. 65.
[2] *New York Times*, 27 April 1998, p. C2.
[3] *Fortune*, 16 October 2000, p. 214.
[4] *Fortune*, 24 May 1999, p. 170.
[5] Ibid., p. 169.

CHAPTER 14

Don't Compete, Change the Game

M any years ago I designed and directed a yearlong training program for psychologists, coaches, and educators on the use of games and sport for self-development. To conduct one of our weekend workshops, I invited Dr. Brian Sutton-Smith, the head of Columbia University's educational psychology department and one of the world's renowned authorities on children's games. During the first few hours of the program, Sutton-Smith had the group play games we had all played as kids: capture the flag, hide-and-seek, Red Rover, Simon says.

It was great fun, but in every game, Dr. Sutton-Smith (are you ready for this?) *cheated*. He kept bending the rules, changing roles, flipping strategies, going outside the boundaries. It was very annoying, so we finally challenged him. His discussion profoundly affected my thinking about competition.

When we compete, he explained, we implicitly agree to play a game the way it has always been played. This means abiding by certain rules, roles, and rituals. Playing by the rules, though it can be fun and challenging, limits the imagination and the opportunity to create something different and better. Kids, on the other hand, are always redesigning the rules to meet the needs of the place, the situation, or their own goals. Kids at play, especially when adults aren't hovering over them, don't conform to the rules and old roles. They are constantly re-creating and reinventing.

TILTING THE PLAYING FIELD

Playing by the same rules and assumptions as everyone else in your industry also limits your opportunities. It keeps you battling head-to-head with your competitors, which leads to massive headaches. The key to gaining a competitive edge is to *use your head to get ahead*. You don't want to play on a level playing field, you want to tilt it in your direction.

"I think a level playing field is a fundamentally wrong notion," says Harvard Business School professor C. V. Prahalad. "Strategy is not about a level playing field . . . it is about a differential advantage. The question then becomes, How do I change the rules of the game in my business so that I hold the high ground on a nonlevel playing field?"[1]

When you focus on beating the other guy, you may offer a few more extras, such as a better service contract or cheaper price. But then your competitor leapfrogs you. This type of thinking keeps you playing the same game, which limits your innovative possibilities as well as the opportunity to significantly differentiate yourself from the competition.

Reinventing the Game

Gaining the edge means not improving on what you do but in reinventing what you do. *Reinvention isn't changing what is, but creating what isn't.* Gary Hamel, the author of *Competing for the Future*, takes it one step further: "I believe that only companies capable of reinventing themselves in their industry in a profound way will be here a decade hence. Today's question is not whether you can reengineer your process but whether you can reinvent the entire business model, like Amazon.com did with books and Enron has done selling energy. Extraordinary successful companies [will] succeed by radically changing the basis of competition in their industries."[2]

A great example of reinvention is Las Vegas. Once a seedy place for gamblers and gangsters, Vegas has transformed itself from a gambling mecca to one of the world's busiest and most spectacular tourist vacation resorts. Its appeal now runs the gamut from families to honeymooners to conventioneers.

Don't Imitate, Innovate

Keeping your eye on the leaders or best in class and trying to benchmark them only makes you a wannabe. By the time you have copied something the leader is doing, they are on to the next innovation—which is why they are leaders. And if you follow the leader, you are a follower who automatically is playing catch-up.

Companies that stay out in front don't imitate, they innovate. They create new markets and reinvent old ones. "We never look at our competitors' products," says Michael Bloomberg. "Why should we assume they know what they are doing? We push our managers to be creative, challenge them not to beat the competition but to rewrite the rules."[3]

The rock band the Grateful Dead not only had millions of "Deadhead" followers but published newsletters and held Deadhead meetings. The Dead's leader, the late Jerry Garcia, once told me, "It's not enough to be the best at what you do, you have to be perceived as the only one who does what you do."

Reinventing Retail

The big successes in these changing, challenging times are those companies that are reinventing themselves and their industry. For instance, it's a misnomer to call recreational equipment company REI's retail space in Seattle a store. This 100,000-square-foot facility, which attracted over 1.5 million visitors in its first year, features, among other things, a glass-enclosed 65-foot climbing pinnacle that is the world's tallest indoor climbing structure, along with an actual biking trail. There's also a rain room where you can test waterproof equipment and a pool filled with brackish water where campers can test water purifiers.

"Retail is moving towards capital E environments," says REI president and CEO Wally Smith. "For us it means education."[4] Reflecting this attitude, Craig Undum, a technician in REI's cycling department, who is also a world-class racer, has formed an REI team that conducts clinics to educate people and get them excited about the sport.

Retail today is also about entertainment. You can shoot hoops at the NBA store, shoot the rapids or evil aliens in the computer store's game department, watch a rock concert at a music store. What's for sale may be the same old stuff—sneakers, books, music—but it's sold with all the pizzazz of a Broadway production. It's no wonder that stores like Woolworth's and Foot Locker had such problems competing.

A Different Shade for Big Blue

One of the most publicized turnarounds in history was a result of IBM's reinventing itself. Back in 1993, when Lou Gerstner, as he says, parachuted into IBM, Big Blue had racked up some $16 billion in losses for the previous three years, and the stock that had once been in triple figures had sunk to the low forties.

The key to this amazing turnaround is that IBM transformed itself from a computer company to a technology and services company in which the Internet plays a key role. Big Blue is now one of the first companies that major corporations come to, not so much for computers, but for information and services relating to gaining a Web presence. IBM's Internet services unit alone is a $3 billion dollar operation and growing at 40 percent per year. And their stock is now trading at about $125. Safe to say that Big Blue is not so blue anymore.

Reinventing a Cup of Joe

Another look at reinvention is the transformation of coffee from the cup of "joe" you once got at the local diner. The majority of credit for this shift goes to Howard Schultz, who has grown a six-store Seattle coffee-bean retailer into Starbucks's billion-dollar megachain of Italian-style coffee bars.

Schultz transformed a plain cup of coffee into a first-rate drink and an entire nation into cappuccino cognoscenti. How did he transform a common cup of joe into a gourmet product? "Our so-called baristas [bartenders] introduce customers to the fine coffees of the world the way wine stewards bring forward fine wines," says Schultz. "They explain the different flavors and . . . introduce great-tasting specialty drinks— brews like decaf doppios and skinny lattes. Eventually patrons become coffee connoisseurs and they keep coming back for another cup."[5]

Dream Merchants

Deregulation has made the financial services industry fiercely competitive. Now banks, stockbrokers, mutual funds, insurance companies, and credit unions are selling virtually the same product to the same client.

To counter this competition, some credit unions are beginning to reinvent themselves by further expanding their offerings. The president of one credit union told me that one of their most popular loans was short-term financing of vacation travel. Spotting an opportunity, an enterprising young staffer in the organization suggested that they expand the game. "As long as we are giving money for vacations, why don't we help our members plan their vacations and even schedule tours for them?"

Taking her advice, they began a partnership with a major travel tour-guide organization and began offering vacation packages and special tours for members. This service not only created an additional profit center for the credit union but was seen as a value-added service for their members. And increasing value is key for member retention.

"We fulfill dreams," the executive director of another credit union told me. "We help people purchase some of the important items they want, like a new house, or vacation home, a boat, or car, or send their kid to college. We not only give them a loan to make the purchase, we provide a service that will help them find the object, negotiate a price, get them insurance, and work out any of the remaining details.

"Since many of our people are baby boomers who are thinking about retirement," he continued, "we also conduct seminars on second careers, or on various retirement options. In essence we have become dream merchants for our members, and our members see us in a whole different light. As a result both our member retention and new member applications are at an all-time high."

HAVING IT BOTH WAYS

One of the biggest needs in the corporate environment today is for information technology (IT) people. People with high-tech skills have their pick of jobs. Companies are offering all types of incentives to get them. As a result, IT staffing firms that do the recruiting and staffing for these jobs are making a killing.

Recognizing a two-sided opportunity, the Judge Group, one of the larger staffing firms, reinvented both themselves and the industry by acquiring Berkeley Computer Training, which provides software and network applications training. This move enabled them to take advantage of two markets. Judge Group now not only finds you people, but trains them as well and saves clients time, money, and hassles. Since Berkeley also trains people in emerging technologies, Judge also retrains people.

The company is also piloting Judge Academy, which helps prospective high-tech employees polish critically needed job skills such as listening, communication, and problem solving.

Teaming Up

This trend of reinventing oneself by acquiring, merging, or partnering with other companies to offer a broader range of products or services is taking place in all areas. Lucent Technologies, North America's biggest maker of communications equipment, has recently bought out International Network Services, a fast-growing consulting company, in order to help large corporate clients install and use their equipment. "The convergence of voice and data is driving tremendous demand for services and support," said Richard McGinn, Lucent's chairman at the time. "Together Lucent and INS will offer customers the industry's deepest portfolio of network planning, design, integration, maintenance, and management solutions."[6]

Little Guys Think Big

Teaming up is also helpful for little guys. I recently worked with manufacturers of wooden roof and floor joists for residential and commercial structures, a niche industry if ever there was one. Their problem is that, as in many industries, the customer's role is changing. Builders and general contractors no longer spend much time on site. They are too busy getting permits, learning new regulations, doing advertising, and working with their salespeople.

These builders need to have one company that can handle all their framing needs, including being a resource for the best materials (be it wood, steel, or laminates) and labor and, most importantly, doing it all faster and cheaper. These new requirements mean that joist manufacturers have to change their game to become building-components design and construction resources. "That's like going from a bike to a jet plane," one manufacturer told me. "We're just little guys."

Affiliating with lumberyards that sold framing materials, paneling, and insulation as well as other types of joists was a first step for these manufacturers in reinventing themselves. They then began working with subcontractors to do the framing. The next step was to hire salespeople to call on the builders to sell the whole package.

This step-by-step reinvention got these folks out of the wooden joist manufacturing business and into something much bigger and more lucrative. Just because you are small, you don't have to think small.

FILLING THE HOLES IN YOUR GAME

We often miss obvious opportunities for reinventing our game. H&R Block has been around for eons, crunching numbers for more than 14 million taxpayers. Yet it took new CEO Frank Salizzoni, a former president of US Airways Group, to spot and solve a very obvious problem. Two thirds of Block's offices closed at the end of the April tax season, but they were still paying rent and the company was losing $83 million in this "off-season."

Building on Block's international name recognition and the fact that they had more field offices than Merrill Lynch, Salizzoni's approach was to reinvent Block from being a tax preparer into a financial services shopping mall helping people with all of their financial affairs: insurance, mortgages, financial planning, and investments. "Our [tax] preparers will tell you that customers are always asking them whether they should start an IRA or how much should they put in their 401(k)," Salizzoni says. "One customer said that Block knew more about him than his spouse did. We're trying to take advantage of that."[7]

Re-creating Your Name

It doesn't take a rocket scientist to see that summer is downtime at ski resorts. To counter this, most of these winter wonderlands offer an abundance of services that span the other seasons, from world-class golf courses, health spas, and mountain biking to gourmet cooking classes, concerts, and music festivals.

I often wonder why they still insist on calling themselves a ski resort. Sure, most of their revenue is probably derived in winter, but maybe that's because nobody thinks about going to a *ski* resort to play *golf*. Reinventing themselves with a change in name and focus might reposition them as a year-round resort and broaden their appeal to the customer.

Where are the holes in your game? What are the downtimes, the off-season, the potential sales with current customers that you are missing? Reinventing yourself, whether by acquiring, partnering, merging, hiring, or even just representing another company, can fill those open spaces and turn your downtimes into peaks.

SMALL CHANGES

Reinventing can sometimes be accomplished with just a small change. John Livingstone was a licensed financial planner whose focus was teaching baby boomers how to plan for their retirement. The competition in financial planning is fierce these days, so he decided to change his focus. Since much of his actual work involved teaching, he decided to make the implicit explicit and reposition himself as an educator.

Livingstone began by scheduling seminars at university extensions. This action resulted in two things. First, the university affiliation increased his credibility and implicitly positioned him as an educator and authority. Second, since these extension universities send out thousands of brochures, they in effect did much of his marketing and helped expand his name recognition. This shift got him out of competing head-to-head with all the banks, stock brokerages, mutual funds, and insurance agents. It also opened up new opportunities for him to do further outreach by giving general seminars to the public. His business became so successful that he had to hire three financial planners to work in his office.

MAKING THE SHIFT

Many software manufactures have reinvented themselves by shifting from selling products to selling solutions. Previously, they were limited to calling on information technology staffers and selling a specific product. Their new consulting-oriented approach enables them to meet with people from all different parts of the client organization, including those at the top. The result is that they become much more knowledgeable about their customers' basic business strategies and can help solve problems and spot new opportunities that they previously didn't know existed.

Half In and Half Out

A problem that some companies encounter occurs when they try to reinvent one aspect of their business strategy but keep utilizing old rules. This is one of the reasons that Xerox stock fell from 60 in July 1999 to approximately 14 one year later.

Xerox shifted their sales strategy from a *product* orientation of selling copiers and printers to a *more consultative* one of solving a customer's total document needs. This change necessitated retraining the salespeople to "forget much of what they used to do,"[8] says David Nadler, chairman of Delta Consulting Group. The new strategy involved calling on different people in different departments with a whole new pitch that was more solution- than product-oriented. The problem, says

Bob Sostilio, a director of Cap Ventures, an industry trend tracker, was that "the new vision was clear but the salespeople were still being commissioned for selling a box."[9]

Changing your game won't work if an integral part of it is still being played by the old rules.

No More Head-to-Head

Don't get caught in the competitive trap. Remember, head-to-head competition only leaves you with headaches. You can tilt the playing field in your direction by reinventing your game, redefining your role with the customer, repositioning yourself, broadening the box, or busting out of it.

)))➡ **KEEP IN MIND**
- ➡ Don't compete, reinvent the game.
- ➡ Don't imitate, innovate.
- ➡ Don't play by someone else's rules, make up your own.
- ➡ Don't sell products, solve problems.

[1] Kriegel, Robert J., and Louis Patler. 1992. *If It Ain't Broke . . . Break It!* (New York: Warner Books).

[2] Gary Hamel. 1999. Leigh Bureau brochure. p. 7. Bridgewater N.J.: Leigh Speakers Bureau.

[3] Ibid.

[4] *Fast Company*, December 1997/January 1998, p. 191.

[5] *Fortune*, 16 March 1998, p. 156.

[6] *New York Times*, 11 August 1999, p. C2.

[7] *Forbes*, 4 May 1998, p. 45.

[8] *Business Week*, 25 October 1999, p. 46.

[9] Ibid.

CHAPTER 15

Look Out of Your Box

Benchmarking the best practices in your industry has become a standard operating procedure. It's also important to attend industry conventions, read journals and newsletters, and network if you want to keep track of the competition and ongoing changes in your business.

But while these things are important, they aren't enough if you want to differentiate yourself and get an edge on the competition. Just keeping tabs on your competitors limits your range of innovation. While following the industry leader may shore up some of your weak points, it won't get you out front. You'll remain a follower, rather than a leader. And by the time you copy the leader, they're going to be on to something else and you'll still be lagging behind.

LOOK OUTSIDE YOUR BUSINESS

To gain a competitive edge, develop new possibilities, and create new opportunities, it's important to broaden your scope. Look outside your business or industry for ideas that you can implement in your own. If, for instance, you are an architect or an accountant and want to develop some creative strategies for generating referrals, you could study techniques used by real estate salespeople.

Before Jack Welch took over GE, the company was known

for ignoring anything that was not invented there. Welch changed all that. Generally acknowledged as the most revered leader in American business, Welch says his company now learns by "thinking outside itself. We have designed a culture that gets people to look outside the company. . . . We're constantly on the search. We brag about learning quick market intelligence from [companies in other fields like] Wal-Mart, Motorola, and Hewlett Packard. From Toyota [we learned] asset management."[1] As has been mentioned, many companies in a variety of industries ranging from automobile to home building have looked to Dell Computer for ideas on managing inventory, manufacturing, and custom marketing. And for years all types of companies have treked to Freeport, Maine, to see how L.L. Bean handles shipping.

Ideas from Oscar®, Autos, and Airlines

The "Gentleman of the Year" extravaganza that GQ magazine initiated several years ago is an example of "looking-out-of-the-box" thinking. These gala events, rewarding celebrities such as John Travolta, Michael Jordan, George Plimpton, Elton John, and Phil Collins, received tremendous media coverage and transformed GQ from a sleepy has-been to the third-hottest magazine in the country last year. Where did they get the idea? From Hollywood's Oscar and Broadway's Tony ceremonies. According to Richard Beckman, GQ's publisher at the time, the brainstorm came by looking out of the publishing industry and to the world of entertainment.

In November 2000, Nike introduced Shox, a line of shoes the company calls its biggest technological innovation since Nike Air shoes made their debut a decade before. Shox has a much bouncier feel than the Air and more spring. In fact, the technology is based on springs—car springs. It is modeled on the technology and materials used in a car's body to cushion the ride. The final design for Shox came from discussions with an automotive parts maker who showed Bruce Kilgore, the shoe's designer, the resilient material used in a bounce jumper, which controls the ride and feel of a car. And now Nike is hoping that bounce jumpers from automobiles will give this new line of shoes an extra bounce.[2]

If indigestion is the only thing you think you can get from airline food, you're wrong. A huge industry was founded as a result of an idea a salesman got from an airline meal. In 1953, C. A. Swanson and Sons, a poultry producer, had a large surplus of turkey meat. The overage was catastrophic since there wasn't enough refrigerated storage room to accommodate it. But on a routine sales call, Swanson executive Gerry Thomas noted the new aluminum trays that the airlines were using for their in-flight meals. Showing the tray to company president Clark Swanson, Thomas pointed to the different compartments of the tray and asked, "What if you put frozen turkey in one compartment, cornbread stuffing in another, and sweet potatoes in another? Stick the whole thing in the oven and in less than half an hour—no fuss, no bother—you've got a meal!"[3] Bingo! The TV dinner was born and now 10 million of them are gobbled down every year.

Learning to Make Dolls from the Auto Industry

The Alexander Doll Co., a maker of children's dolls, based in Harlem, New York, utilized the same approach in order to streamline their operation. Rather than move their production overseas like much of their competition, the company looked overseas to the Japanese auto industry for ideas. Studying Toyota's lean production methods led them to totally reorganize their systems. Instead of having workers individually producing parts, they emulated Toyota's production team approach. Orders are now filled in one to two weeks instead of two months. And sales in this company, which was headed for bankruptcy in 1995, rose to $32 million three years later.

HUD Huddles

You don't have to be a high-level business consultant to realize that there is enormous waste in government. Former Speaker of the House Newt Gingrich, in a speech to business executives, said he thought the Pentagon had so much waste that it should be reduced to a triangle. I always recommend that both nonprofit and public sector organizations look "out of their cubicle," to the private sector, for ideas on how to streamline their operation and provide better service for the public.

Andrew Cuomo, secretary of HUD, the Housing and Urban Development agency, reduced the average time it took to process home insurance claims from one month to two days by studying the operations of commercial banks. Additionally, seeing how banks were offering better service with fewer people and fewer buildings, Cuomo consolidated HUD's widely scattered administrative sites into a handful of automated processing centers. And just as banks have transformed their funereal environments, Cuomo has reconfigured his street-level offices. HUD's "Next Door" center blends the corner bank with the local coffee shop atmosphere, featuring lots of windows, exposed beams, and inviting upholstered chairs.

Looking Global to Learn Local

After a period of declining food quality, shrinking market share, and a generally falling stock price, McDonald's is back on track. One reason for this recovery is that the fast-food giant is looking outside the country to their own international franchises, which have been incredibly successful even in poor economies. Unlike McDonald's in the United States, their foreign counterparts don't sell only Big Macs and fries. In many countries the Golden Arches offer flexible menus that cater to local palates.

The McDonald's menu in Jakarta, for instance, includes rice as well as french fries. In Seoul they sell roast pork on a bun and garlic soy sauce. "McCafés," providing coffee blended for local tastes, are a big hit with customers in Vienna. And strolling down the Champs Elysées, you can see people sitting outside sipping wine under the Golden Arches. Looking to their foreign counterparts, McDonald's realized that all business is local. I recently saw a Golden Arches in New York City offering bagels and cream cheese for breakfast. How about McCappuccino in LA or blackened McCatfish in New Orleans?

Follow the Money Guys

Hospitals, these days, are being squeezed like never before due to continually shrinking reimbursement income and increasing numbers of surgical procedures being done on an outpatient basis. The common response to these reduced revenues is to "bring in the hatchet" and cut costs. But cutting costs also cuts quality care and staff motivation.

The one near certainty in the unpredictable world of health care is that reimbursements aren't going to increase and outpatient procedures aren't going to return to the hospital. It's imperative therefore that hospitals find sources of income that aren't tied into reimbursements.

One place hospitals could look to for ideas is financial institutions, which have experienced the same type of problem. Their primary source of money in the past was net interest income, the spread between the rate they borrow cash from the Fed and the rate they lend it to you and me. Then along came deregulation, which meant increased competition in financial services from more aggressive competitors such as mutual funds, brokerage houses, insurance companies, and the e-guys. So banks, facing increased competition and decreased revenue, began having a real tough time.

Rather than just sit there and suffer or take to the hatchet, banks began changing their game to find new sources of revenue. Partnering, merging, and consolidating enabled them to offer all sorts of new financial packages and services, such as financial consulting, stocks, and insurance, and are now looking to get into the real estate business. As a result the old traditional source of revenue, the net interest income, has become less important.

Hiring out of the Box

Recruiting and keeping good people is one of the biggest problems businesses of all sizes face these days. One way to find good people is to look outside the traditional places. Electronic Scriptorium in Leesburg, Virginia, went far outside the box to find people for the painstaking job of creating electronic databases for online companies, libraries, and academic institutions. They hired nuns and monks because they are diligent, discreet, and love to have clean, quiet, well-paying jobs that don't interfere with prayer and meditation. "The work is in keeping with monastic tradition," says Edward Leonard, president of the company.[4] Maybe someone is looking over his shoulder, because revenues are growing at an annual rate of 30 percent.

Rockin' and Rollin' to Success

Steve Hoffman, a Ph.D. in marine biology, and one of the founders of Home Account, an online financial services company, told me about a patent he claimed by transferring his knowledge from one area into another. As a marine biologist, Hoffman had spent as many as five to six hours a day underwater gathering data. To transcribe his notes while underwater, he had to use a tape recorder in a Plexiglas box and an awkward mouthpiece, which was very clumsy. It was also time-consuming, because after he dried off, he had to spend hours entering his data into a computer.

Drawing on his experience as a guitarist, he invented a touch-based underwater keyboard that would enter information into an on-land PC in real time. The key to the invention was his idea that he could enter data by curling his hands around the keyboard and fingering the keys, as he would his guitar.[5]

Orpheus Ascending

Can you imagine future executives learning from people making $30,000 a year? It's happening. Graduate students at the Zicklin School of Business at Baruch College, in New York City, attend sessions on leadership led by Orpheus, a Grammy-winning orchestra that is an annual fixture at Carnegie Hall.

Orchestras normally have structures similar to those of corporations. The conductor is king and his word is law. As Renee Jolees, an Orpheus violinist says, "When you play with a conductor . . . [you] sit there and do what you're told."[6] Orpheus's success is accomplished *without* an onstage boss. All the members give advice, hash out decisions, and work together to develop creative solutions.

In this era of corporate downsizing, many institutions, including giant Kraft Foods and several major hospitals, are learning a lot from this orchestra that has no layers. "Orpheus gives every individual an opportunity to lead," says business director Harvey Seifter. "But it also creates an imperative that everyone pull together."[7] Companies from all over the world are looking and listening to Orpheus to help them duplicate the culture, connection, and teamwork of this orchestra.

Flying Butlers

You can also bring in people from other industries to offer you a different perspective than your own. For instance, what does a Broadway production have in common with an airline beyond the fact that both have seats? One airline brought in a Broadway producer for a brainstorming session. "We are a theater with wings," one of the executives said, "so why not learn from theater people?" The airline also brought in a butler to teach their people about personal service.

Looking Outside for Partners

Ever play the video game Pac-Man, in which one entity gobbles up others? Well, Pac-Manning is happening big-time in business these days. Big companies are gobbling up either other large companies or several smaller ones in an effort to make themselves even stronger. But at the same time that these companies are consolidating, merging, and acquiring others to grow larger, they are also trying to get smaller, quicker, and more flexible by outsourcing everything that is not a core strength.

Everyone seems to be outsourcing. This strategy of farming out certain areas of your own company to streamline your operation or gain a strategic advantage is growing at more than 25 percent a year and is now a $180 billion business worldwide. More than one third of all companies with over $50 million in sales outsource one or more areas of their company.

Many companies even outsource parts of their operation to a competitor. Rather than manufacturing their own components, Dell Computer agreed to buy $16 billion worth of equipment from—guess who?—IBM. Crazy? Why should Dell do what IBM can do better and cheaper? Working with IBM has proven so satisfactory that Dell just signed a seven-year $6 billion pact with them to provide technical support for their customers.

Outsourcing isn't limited to megacorporations. Several colleagues of mine who give over seventy speeches a year at corporate meetings and association conventions outsource their total administration and marketing to a speakers' bureau. "Who needs all the headaches of running a business and marketing? Now all I have to focus on is my speeches. They do the rest. And you know something?" one of them told me. "It's actually costing me less to use them than to have my own office."

"Why not outsource the government too?" asked Geoff Baehr, chief of network design at Sun Microsystems, with a little tongue in cheek. "You could outsource your commando operations and border-guard jobs to the Russians. You could have the Indians keep your country's books . . . the Swiss run your customs service . . . the Germans run your central bank . . . the Italians design all your shoes . . . the British run your high schools. . . ."[8]

)))⟶ **KEEP IN MIND**

⟶ Look "outside" for new ideas, partners, and possibilities.

⟶ Don't restrict your reading to industry rags and business publications.

⟶ The further out of your box you look, the more innovative the possibilities.

[1] *Fortune*, 11 January 1999, p. 163.

[2] *New York Times*, 12 November 2000, p. B4.

[3] *Fortune Small Business*, February/March 2000, p. 116.

[4] *Fortune*, 27 September, 1999, p. 262.

[5] Steve Hoffman, conversation with the author, 30 June 2000.

[6] Ibid.

[7] *New York Times*, 10 November 1999, p. C14.

[8] Thomas Friedman, *The Lexus and the Olive Tree* (New York: Anchor Books, 2000), p. 53.

CHAPTER 16

Get Out of Your Box

A major corporate honcho recently told me that the one thing he most hated to see was the shape of a manager's butt matching the shape of his office chair. In his best-selling book *In Search of Excellence*, Tom Peters introduced the notion of MBWA—management by walking around. Great idea. By now it's old news, but it's still critical to get out and see what is going on in your business—to talk to your employees as well as your customers.

Let's take this concept a step further. I'm not talking about merely getting out of your office. If you want to find some cutting-edge ideas that might change the shape of what you are doing and how you are doing it, it's important not only to get out of your company, but to get out of the business world altogether. Investigate places that have nothing to do with your industry. The further you extend the parameters of your search, the better ideas you'll find.

BOYS IN THE HOOD

Want some guides for getting out of your box? Try taking a quick trip with Glen Caplin and John Eckstein, Jr., the co-founders of Don't Think Twice Promotion and Marketing. They developed a technique called immersion to help executives "get hip" to the next big fads. Immersion is essentially a guided interactive tour of "the hood"—the place where many of the trends start.

One such tour for six Ford Motor executives began with "a 7 A.M. visit to Westinghouse High School in downtown Brooklyn, moved on to a hip-hop clothing store, a high-end car stereo retailer, and a round of meetings with marketing executives from urban-music and street-fashion companies, and ended up with a stroll down Fordham Road, the Bronx's main see-and-be-seen drag."[1]

In meetings and talks with the kids, "we ask them to tell us what brands they think are hot and why," says Caplin. "And on Fordham Road the guys from Ford can see all the kids' rides."[2] Of course, prior to each immersion session, Caplin teaches his executives some appropriate slang and important tips, one of which is to forget the suit and the wing tips.

Caplin admits that some of the executives are initially taken aback by the experience. "But without fail they all end up getting into it, talking to the kids, even using some slang."[3] After Ford's first immersion, they scheduled two more. In fact, Ford CEO Jacques Nasser is now interested in flying in for one of these sessions. Caplin said, "We're ready to schedule him anytime . . . as long as he's cool and not wearing shiny shoes and a blazer."[4]

Hit the Beach

Where did you think Nokia got the idea for its highly successful line of rainbow-colored phones? Not at a strategy session but by going to the beach, Muscle Beach in Venice, California, to be exact, where people's outfits were totally color coordinated from sunglasses to makeup to hats, shorts, and even skates. Recognizing that cell phones could be a fashion accessory, as well as a communications device, they introduced color phones. Bingo!

GETTING TO THEIR MINDS THROUGH THEIR STOMACHS

Newbury Comics opened its first music and novelty store in the 1970s at a time when only banks sold CDs. To keep in tune with changing tastes, Newbury marketing director Amy Dorfman regularly takes small groups of twenty-somethings out to dinner and gives them a fifty-dollar gift certificate. While chowing down, she grills them on everything from customer service to the latest lingo, products, and gizmos. Based on the feedback she got after just a few of these info-thons, the company shifted its whole advertising strategy from newspapers and radio to movie theaters and buses, where young shoppers are more likely to see them. Dorfman's advice: "Listen to your customers even when their mouths are full."[5]

To get the jump on some new trends, you gotta go where the trends are born. And that ain't happening at the water cooler.

CRUISE SHIPS AND PIT STOPS

Rather than looking to other hospitals, a large Southern California hospital, wanting to be known for great patient care, began studying industries that specialized in pampering the customer. Managers were sent to spas, resort hotels, and cruise ships and returned bursting with patient-care ideas. Some of the "out-of-the-hospital-box" ideas that they implemented included valet parking, automated check-in, and special programs and entertainment. They even went so far as to repaint the inside of the building, play soft music in the halls, and provide new uniforms for the staff.

These changes were so unusual for a hospital that they were featured in the Sunday editions of several Southern California newspapers. Banner headlines read INTENSIVE CARING

HOSPITAL. This institution went from being rated eighteenth to third in their area in less than two years.

One of the most profitable airlines in the United States for several years has been Southwest. A David in a field of Goliaths, Southwest has broken all the rules. They give passengers a number instead of a seat, a bag of peanuts rather than a meal, and their flight attendants give instructions in everything from rap to rhyme.

Southwest also has the fastest turnaround of any airline. Where do you think they got ideas for quick turnarounds? If you're thinking United or Delta, try again! If you're thinking fast food or Federal Express, you're on the right track. Speaking of track, that's where they went. To the *Indy 500*—where a pit stop to change tires, fuel up, and clean the windshield takes approximately twelve seconds.

Other examples: A group of top managers for an insurance company went to a comedy shop to learn to be better presenters. Bank managers for a large Midwestern bank were sent to work with car dealers to learn to be more aggressive.

GETTING OUT

Everything is grist for the mill. Anything outside of your immediate environment can feed your creativity, nourish your imagination, and broaden your perspective. On his honeymoon trip to Oregon in the early 1900s, Edwin Oliver, an engineer and surveyor who had been working for two years to find better and cheaper methods of extracting gold from mill tailings, found his answer. The operation he saw on a chance visit to a paper mill led him to invent the first continuous drum filtration system, which then became standard equipment for all gold mines of that era.[6]

The natural world has much to teach us about creating work environments where everything is both independent and interdependent. Physics and astronomy can teach us how to balance order and chaos. Gardening is an incredible metaphor for growth.

In his book *Surfing the Edge of Chaos*, former Stanford Business School professor Richard Pascale, who is now an Oxford University fellow, tells us, "Corporations shouldn't look to the machine as a model when adapting to challenging market conditions. They should look to nature, which provides concrete examples of how to evolve and thrive."[7]

You can get great ideas just going on a hike. A Swiss scientist began wondering about all the burrs that were sticking to him during a walk in the woods. His experience led him to invent Velcro.

It's long been known that travel broadens the mind. I don't mean going to Paris for a business trip where you stay in a luxury hotel and speak English. Different cultures have much to teach us. Seeing how the natives of an area live exposes you to ideas and practices that can open your mind to new possibilities. As I mentioned earlier, Clarence Birdseye founded the frozen food industry and made a fortune from an idea he got watching Eskimos freeze fish while he was on vacation in Alaska.

Show Biz

Business books and motivational speakers have long used sport, military, politics, religion, and high adventure as metaphors and sources for ideas and philosophies about how to succeed in business. There are books about how everyone from George Washington to Jesus to Attila the Hun would lead an organization.

Bruce Payne, who has been teaching leadership at Duke University for three decades and received Duke's Distinguished Undergraduate Teaching Award, has a different idea about how to teach his students about leadership. Payne takes them to New York City, where they spend more than four months going to Broadway shows, operas, ballet, and art galleries. (Think there's much of a waiting line to get into that class?)

Payne's charges meet with actors, such as two-time Academy Award–winner Kevin Spacey, directors, producers, dancers, writers, painters, and just about anyone else that is doing anything in the arts. "In a new world of corporate America, everybody is worried about how to achieve excellence in smaller and flatter organizations," says Payne. "That means finding styles of leadership that work well with smart, self-respecting professionals. The people who succeed in the arts these days are people who have solved the problem. They know how to coach, they know how to encourage, they know how to praise, and they know how to love. And they know how to express a vision that excites rather than intimidates."[8]

As Annie Oakley in *Annie Get Your Gun* sang, "There's no business like show business."

Getting Arty

Nike Town, with its huge wall of fifty screens featuring Michael Jordan and the other Nike flyers, is on the cutting edge of retail entertainment and can give you lots of ideas about how to display products and entertain customers. But if you want to open your mind to possibilities, the Guggenheim's got a wall exhibit with *one thousand* screens, each linked to a computer. The exhibit is supposed to mimic the brain. A big thought, for instance, takes up seven hundred screens, and other thoughts, such as those about sex and eating, are always pulsing (clever machine). And get this, that exhibit is *ten years old!*

"Contemporary art is the R&D lab of the future," says Steve Zades, chairman and CEO of LHC, a hot creative think tank. "I see the intersection of business and art as the new frontier."[9] With this in mind, Zades opens up the minds of both his employees and clients by taking them to museums like the Guggenheim, the theater, and art galleries.

PRESENTATION SCHOOLING

Getting out of your box can provide new insights on how to improve personal performance and productivity as well as creativity. " 'Low C' was the grade I got after my first client presentation as an advertising account executive. That stands for low credibility and low confidence," Alex Kroll, the creative director who went on to become chairman of Young & Rubicam, told me. I was capital C—crushed.

I realized that if I was going to succeed in that business or any other, I would have to become a better presenter. On a whim, I decided to take a course in improvisation and theater games. It was such an empowering experience and so much fun that I followed it up with an acting course.

In these classes, I grew comfortable and more confident in front of a group. I learned the importance of body language and how to stay focused and not get distracted when things weren't going as planned. I also learned how to tell a good story and how to win over a potentially hostile audience. The skills I learned in those classes helped me enormously, not only in that job but in my current work as a keynote speaker. In fact, I still take theater workshops to polish my skills and, more importantly, have fun.

A major asset in any job, especially one demanding leadership qualities, is to be an effective and inspiring communicator. If you are successful, you will be called on to conduct meetings, give presentations, and make speeches. It's important to be poised and have charisma in order to motivate and inspire your audience, whether it's five people or five hundred. I have seen many intellectually brilliant executives, and most likely so have you, who leave an audience yawning and looking at their watches.

Wall Street Applause

Steve Panken, a partner in Enzyme Systems, a biochemical company, gave me an example of the value of being a great presenter in his industry. "There were two companies in the medical research field with similar capitalization structures and similar backlogs of products. Both were dynamic companies, both brought public by venture capitalists. In other words," Panken told me, "they were almost mirror images of each other.

"The difference between the two was that the CEO of one was a great presenter, whereas the other was a typical scientist, bland, dull, and boring. The share price of the company with the dynamic CEO was 40, whereas the other company's stock was selling at 10."[10]

Research shows that the content of your message in a presentation represents less than 10 percent of its effect. That doesn't mean that you can present fluff in a great way and succeed. But the person who is a great presenter has a definite edge. Taking an acting or improvisation course will help you develop presence and poise on the platform.

BECOMING A GOOD LEARNER

With everything changing at breakneck speed these days, it is critical for us all to be adept learners if we want to survive, much less succeed. In fact, leaders and managers are being told that the model of the company that will succeed in these chaotic times is the learning organization.

Stressing the importance of learning, Lawrence Bossidy, one of the preeminent leaders in American business, tells his people, "Don't come in here on Saturday and Sunday unless something special is going on, because all you're going to do is become a bore. I mean, do something, music or whatever you like, but for heaven's sake, grow."[11]

From Sports to Business

Physical activities offer an opportunity to gain personal insights about how to facilitate your learning at work. When I was conducting Inner Skiing workshops, I noticed that people often played a sport in the same manner they performed in other areas of their life. As a result, I developed a process of transferring lessons gained from one activity to other areas.

At our après-ski meetings, I would ask the group to reflect on their skiing that day and see what they had learned. Jane Laidlaw, an interior decorator for a major department store in Los Angeles, looked up with surprise, saying, "Today I realized why I can't seem to get off the intermediate slope and ski the expert runs. It's not that I don't have the skills. I'm afraid of falling and looking bad. So I stay in my comfort zone."

I then asked Jane to transfer that insight to her life to see if it was apropos. After thinking for a minute, she said, "You're right! My job is safe and boring but I'm scared to go out on my own for the same reason. I'm afraid to fail and look bad and that people will think I'm foolish."

Bob's Better Benches

I recently took up woodworking and have made several pieces of furniture. It's been an exhilarating experience. But in the process, I had to learn much more than woodworking skills.

I have always hated taking time to read directions or plans when learning anything new. Naturally I carried these tendencies into my woodworking, thinking, as I normally do, that I would learn as I went along. And I did. I burned out a motor, ruined several saw blades and numerous pieces of wood, and almost lost a finger. I soon learned that my impatience actually impeded my learning and caused me to make more mistakes. This experience taught me to read directions, plan my work carefully, and, as my neighbor John Faats, a rocket engineer, taught me, measure twice so you only have to cut once—and not your finger.

Turning Experts to Beginners

Many managers fail to develop their people because they aren't good teachers and coaches. One reason for this is that they don't identify, and therefore don't connect, with the person they are trying to coach.

When I trained ski instructors, I found that most were great skiers but poor teachers. Why? Because they had learned to ski when very young and had forgotten how they learned. It was very difficult for them to identify with their students or relate to the experiences that beginners were having. The result was an industry filled with bad teachers and frustrated learners.

So we took these ski instructors to the tennis court, where we had them play with their opposite hand! Being out of their comfort zone caused them to feel awkward and unsure of themselves. And like the beginning skiers they were teaching on the slopes, they worried about making mistakes and looking foolish.

Turning these experts into beginners was of tremendous value. Having now gone through experiences similar to those of their students helped these ski instructors empathize with them and become much better teachers.

Kicking Butt

Many years ago I studied aikido. No, I wasn't trying to be another Bruce Lee or Jean-Claude Van Damme. The goal of most martial arts isn't to be able to beat up someone. It's to learn how to remain centered—calm, cool, and in control when under pressure. The test for a black belt was to be able to remain centered when five guys were attacking you and to use the throws you were taught.

You're probably not being attacked by five guys at work. But I bet you have more things than that coming at you that you have to handle. Centering techniques from the martial arts will help you think more clearly and perform under pressure with less stress and more composure in other areas of your life.

The "B" Word

Four years after Julie Morgenstern started Task Masters it was a huge success, with clients such as American Express, Bear Stearns, Merrill Lynch, and Chase Manhattan Bank signing on as clients. But Morgenstern felt like she was overwhelmed and didn't have a life. Deciding she needed an outlet, she chose dance.

"Once a week I would go to a swing dance class. Suddenly I had more time on my hands and was more energized during the week. I moved through my tasks at lightning speed. When your life is as unbalanced as mine was, you feel like you don't have time to breathe," says Morgenstern, who is also the author of *Organizing from the Inside Out*.[12] "But when you take time to rebalance your life everything gets easier."[13]

From Left Brain to Right

As I mentioned earlier, most of us spend a good deal of our time using the *left* side of our brain, which controls rational thinking. But innovative thinking involves the *right* hemisphere of the brain. And as with any underused muscle in your body, if this part of your mind isn't being used, it will atrophy and not be available when you need it.

Use it or lose it. Painting, sculpting, singing, and dancing, for instance, are great ways to exercise the right side of your brain. An engineer I know recently took up freehand drawing and told me it has helped him become a much better problem solver. He says, "It has taught me to see the obvious, what is really in front of me. The best ideas are always right in front of our noses. But we don't see them because we literally over-look them."

You can't tell when that "aha" will strike. I recently read about a man who is revolutionizing the concrete-block building industry with an idea he got from playing with Legos with his kids.

But don't take up these activities just because they'll help you at work. Most of the activities I have mentioned are *fun*. And nothing will enhance your creativity and productivity and your quality of life as much as adding more fun, joy, and beauty to your life.

➠➠ **KEEP IN MIND**

➠ Get out and get inspired by art exhibits, theater, opera, ballet, and concerts.

➠ Look to nature for inspiration and metaphors.

➠ Take a course not related to your job.

➠ Utilize the right side of your brain as well as the left.

➠ Get out from behind your desk—it provides only a limited view.

[1] *The New Yorker*, 23–30 August 1999, p. 67.

[2] Ibid.

[3] Ibid.

[4] Ibid.

[5] *Fortune*, 3 April 2000, p. 264.

[6] *Nevada County Business News*, October 2000, p. 12.

[7] *American Way*, 15 October 2000, p. 116.

[8] Ibid.

[9] *Fast Company*, October 1999, p. 56.

[10] Steve Panken, conversation with the author, 15 March 2000.

[11] *New York Times*, 10 October 1999, p. Bu13.

[12] Julie Morgenstern, *Organizing from the Inside Out* (New York: Henry Holt, 1998).

[13] *Fast Company*, November 1999, p. 170.

CHAPTER 17

Look Back

I f you don't learn from the past, you will be destined to re-peat it," philosopher George Santayana advised us. Peter Brooke called "the unchallenged genius of theatre cre-ation" by the *London Evening Standard,* has produced operas and plays all over the world. Brooke says that "to find the way forward you sometimes have to go back to the great works of the past."[1] In business as well as in the arts today, many very successful and innovative companies are taking the advice of Santayana and Brooke and are not only looking back and learning from the past but are actually trying to repeat it.

THE GOOD OLD DAYS

The past I am referring to is not the Middle Ages but the near past—about fifty years ago. It's the time of *Leave It to Beaver* and *Ozzie and Harriet,* when people were more relaxed. Work in those days was something you did in order to live, as op-posed to now, when people are living to work.

In this good-old-days environment, businesses gave great service not because it was going to give them a competitive edge, but because they genuinely cared. Those were times when everyone from the clothing store to the barbershop re-membered your name, your preference, and your last pur-chase. The food market and the dry cleaners delivered, and the place where you filled up your car with gas really was a service station. In this age of customer service, many businesses are now looking back to the near past for ideas on how to better serve their customers. In fact, Smith Barney brags that they work the "old-fashioned way."

The New World

Food markets, dry cleaners, and even auto dealers are delivering what you want, when and how you want it. The service station really does serve you. You can get a cup of coffee or a cappuccino and even do some shopping while your car is being worked on. Maybe the proprietor of the business doesn't remember your name or what you ordered, but his computer does. And maybe they don't have time to send you a personalized thank-you, but there are lots of services that will do it for them and even include a beautiful gift.

The Pied Piper

Speaking of the good old days, I can remember when the Good Humor man came to our block every evening to sell ice cream, the milkman and iceman delivered to our door, and our doctor made house calls. Well, Snap-on Tools, the giant of the automotive tool market with over $1.3 billion in sales and a 60 percent market share, does business that same "old-fashioned" way. Each of their six thousand sales representatives climb into their white Snap-on vans and visit each of their two hundred to three hundred customers once a week.

"When the Snap-on guy comes, he is like the Pied Piper," says Ray Magliozzi, a garage owner in Cambridge, Massachusetts, who is better known as cohost of the National Public Radio broadcast program *Car Talk*. "His van is filled with those real things that make you happy."[2]

Snap-on chairman Robert Cornog says, "It looks archaic, but instead of real estate [a store] on the corner with fixed costs of people, taxes, and overhead, we have a very powerful business out there at point of sale."[3]

Basket Parties

The Longaberger Company of Newark, Ohio, is America's largest manufacturer of all types of handwoven baskets from picnic baskets to laundry baskets. Longaberger sells the baskets by emulating the old Tupperware parties in which women would come to your house and present the line to you and your friends. Longaberger's term for their parties is "home shows," in which a woman gets another woman to host a basket party and invites friends, relatives, and neighbors. The result of all these basket parties is sales of over forty thousand baskets a day, almost half a billion dollars worth. As *New Yorker* reporter James Suroweicki writes, "Somehow a company selling a nineteenth-century product in a mid-twentieth-century manner has turned out to be a master in the twenty-first century. . . . The home party, that campy relic of the Cleaver years, may be the ideal mechanism for winning the hearts and minds of American consumers."[4]

Turning Back the Clock

Some establishments aren't just looking to the past for ideas but are actually re-creating those good old days. Remember when the neighborhood drugstore not only had a friendly pharmacist who knew your name and gave personal advice for your kids' measles but also had a soda counter selling floats, malts, and egg creams? Well, you can take a trip back in time by visiting the Fair Oaks Pharmacy and soda fountain in Pasadena, California. Michael and Meredith Miller restored this store to its glorious past by adding an antique soda fountain as well as other authentic touches from Archie and Jughead days. At this great "old place" you can get all the creamy treats from your childhood, if your current diet allows, and both the soda jerk and the pharmacist make house calls. So you can get both your medicine and your reward for taking it delivered to your bedside.

Like many small mom-and-pop operations, Fair Oaks, which was started in 1915, was being threatened by the big chains popping up all around them. In fact, a giant Rite-Aid opened across the street. But though Fair Oaks may remind you of the past, its bottom line is up-to-date, with annual revenues of $2.5 million, almost 50 percent more than the average independent drugstore.

Retro Is Cool

Many businesses are looking to the old days for ideas about new products in everything from clothing to cars. My son and his Generation X friends are dressing in what resemble the clothes I used to wear but threw out because they were no longer cool. Retro is in. It's now hip. And retro is not only cool in clothes. There's even a cultural swing back to habits and products of the old days, like martinis, and cigars.

How about the latest retro rage in cool cars—the VW Beetle, a throwback to the old style that pervaded the sixties and seventies. Going back even further, what would you have if you updated the old World War II army jeep, trading the all-aluminum multifuel engine for a standard gasoline motor, dropping the jeep's independent, fully articulated (read bumpy) suspension for solid axles and leaf springs, and then sprucing up the interior and exterior with things like pile carpets, styled steel wheels, and cool roll bars? That's right—the most popular car on the market, the sport utility vehicle. Makes me wonder if the next trend in cars is going to be fins and dual carbs—oh yeah, they don't have carburetors anymore.

In my college days only real cowboys wore Levi's. The casual pants were khakis. But then they became very uncool— too preppy for most. But look around now. Everyone is wearing what we used to call khakis, and they come in all colors from tan to black. Only now they are called Dockers. And Levi-Strauss is selling over a billion dollars' worth of them.

Fashion designers also look to the past. Yves Saint Laurent, the designer whose radical work in the 1970s got women to wear pants, miniskirts, tuxedos, wide-brimmed hats, and men's shoes, got many of his styles from the 1940s and before. And *New York Times* fashion correspondent Dana Thomas writes that "today's hot young designers like Prada, Gaultier, Michael Kors and Tom Ford are referring to the late sixties and early seventies just as Saint Laurent and his peers looked back thirty years earlier for inspiration."[5]

Recycling Old Hits

TV and movie executives are constantly looking back to see what worked in the past and are trying to give it a new spin.

"Every top ten show has been seen before. The trick is to repackage and contemporize to make a modern hit. *ER* is derived from the likes of *Medical Center. Ally McBeal* is *The Mary Tyler Moore Show*,"[6] says Peter Roth, the president of Warner Bros. Television. Roth admits to paging through television nostalgia books and circling the shows that could be profitably updated. One of his proudest achievements was when, at Fox, he "circled *Kolchak: the Night Stalker* and . . . out of that came *The X-Files*."[7]

The Greening of Black-and-White

By reaching back in time, the photography industry looks as if it has found a way to stimulate sluggish sales. After years of being outdated, black-and-white photography is booming. Market leader Eastman Kodak predicts a significant increase in black-and-white film this year, the first rise since the early seventies.

All the big guys are getting back into it. Kodak introduced a new developing process for black-and-white film that cuts costs to consumers. Polaroid recently introduced its first new instant black-and-white film in almost thirty years. And Kon-ica came out with a black-and-white disposable camera.

Steven Gross, a Chicago wedding photographer who works only in black-and-white, says his business has nearly doubled in the past year. But, he says ruefully, it's now be-come the fashion and lots of other photographers are jump-ing into it.

Even big marketers are getting into this "old" new look. Innovative marketing companies like IBM, Gatorade, and Calvin Klein are using black-and-white in their TV commer-cials and magazine ads. "Using black-and-white is a way of standing out and getting attention," says Cincy Alston, VP of development for Gatorade.[8]

Speaking of super hip and super successful, Abercrombie & Fitch has grown tenfold by cracking one of the toughest markets in retailing—the maddeningly fickle teen and college set. Over two hundred A&F stores have black-and-white pho-tos by fashion photographer Bruce Weber decorating the walls. Their quarterly magalog, a combination magazine and catalogue, is also filled with black-and-white.

The idea of creating contrast by using black-and-white to reflect the past or tough times has also been recently used in films like *Pleasantville* and *Saving Private Ryan.*

Summing up this trend of going back to the good old days, David Apicella, the executive creative director at Ogilvy & Mather, the giant international advertising agency that repre-sents Kodak, says, "Sometimes what's fresh and new is what has been around and fallen out of favor."[9] That's a good les-son for all of us looking for "new" ideas.

Making Bread the Good Old-Fashioned Way

Want to make a lot of bread? Well, there's a company that makes bread literally by making bread. Rather than crystal-gazing into the future, Dan Sterling got his idea from an Old World habit. While studying in Europe, he became hooked on hearth-baked bread and the daily ritual of buying it fresh from the oven. He figured that once people sampled fresh, all-natural bread, they wouldn't go back to the mass-produced prepackaged stuff, even if it does, to quote the old Wonder Bread slogan, "build strong bodies in twelve ways."

His company, Breadsmith, a Milwaukee-based bakery chain, centers on this Old World premise. And pardon the pun, but their pile of dough is rising. The tendency of Americans to stock up on groceries weekly rather than shop daily hasn't been an obstacle. About 40 percent of Breadsmith's customers shop three times a week. The irresistible scent of fresh bread lures people into the store. And once inside, the bakers encourage you to sample the fresh baked loaves, which include basics like rustic Italian bread, French peasant loaf, and sourdough, as well as one of their daily specialties.

Breadsmith isn't a flash in the pan. The romance of the Old World bakery seems to be working. Starting with one store in 1993, they're now approaching fifty.

Speaking of bread, Lionel Poilane sells the most famous bread in Paris, which he developed by tapping into the memories of the oldest bakers in the country. As a result his bread is decidedly old school, thick, chewy, and dark with fire-tinged flavor like the old regional breads of the poor people. Poilane sells about fifteen thousand of these loaves every day. "There are many ways to solve a problem," says Poilane. "In baking, people are always looking for new ways to make new things. Using old ways is a glorious way to make things new. The man with the best future is the one with the longest memory."[10]

New Old Ideas

Most of the companies that successfully used something from the past didn't merely repeat the idea. Rather, they usually combined something old with something new, taking something from the past and modernizing it, and giving it a new twist.

Some ways to use the past to get fresh new ideas are to watch old movies, read magazines from the 1920s and 1930s, and talk to older people. Remember your own experience of growing up and some of the things you did to earn a few bucks. I used to supplement my allowance when I was a kid by packing and carrying people's shopping bags home from the supermarket. Now there are successful businesses based solely on that practice. With change happening at such an incredibly rapid pace these days, some of the examples in this book that were new and innovative at the time of writing may already be dated and ready for recycling. To make your dough rise in the future, add a dash of the past. Combining something old with something new can help you to make better "bread."

⟫➡ KEEP IN MIND

➠ The past can be a resource for the future.
➠ Recycling old favorites can lead to new ones.
➠ You can move forward by looking back.

[1] *London Evening Standard*, 28 November 1997, p. 28.
[2] *Your Company*, February/March 1999, p. 52.
[3] Ibid.
[4] *New Yorker*, 9 April 2001, p. 42.
[5] *New York Times Magazine*, 30 April 2000, p. 69.
[6] Ibid.
[7] Ibid.
[8] Alex Klein, "In Photography, Black and White Turns Green," *Wall Street Journal*, p. B1.
[9] Ibid.
[10] *Fast Company*, March 2001, p. 165.

CHAPTER 18

Listen Down

Attention! In the Marine Corps, when an officer entered our barracks, the sergeant would admonish us to "listen up!" In the armed forces, as in the corporate world, the "word" always comes down from the top.

Most organizations operate with this mentality. Obviously, some things must come from the top. But your organization limits its innovative possibilities if it operates solely from a top-down, "listen-up" mentality. One of the best ways to find creative ideas and new solutions to old problems is to *listen down*.

The most overlooked and underrated source of innovative ideas is your staff. Many of the best suggestions for new products and breakthrough service come from people who deal directly with your customer, those who talk to them day in and out and hear their wishes, desires, and complaints. Similarly many great ideas for streamlining productivity, cutting costs, and eliminating time-consuming and money-wasting practices come not from the supervisors but from the people who work on the line.

Retail stores whose main customers are young people are often managed by someone who has a great deal of experience. The problem is that these managers are often much older than their customers. But guess what? Their salespeople aren't. They're individuals and can understand and relate to the customers much better. So guess where you are going to get your best ideas?

"No leader can possibly have all the answers," says Steve Miller, group managing director of Royal Dutch Shell. "The actual solutions about how best to meet the challenges of the moment have to be made by the people closest to the action."[1]

Rakesh Gangwal, recently promoted to chief executive of the US Airways Group, said, "I love it when front-line employees come up with ideas, because I know they are the things that generally work."[2]

Gary Hamel says, "Despite all the aphorisms to the contrary, change does not start at the top." In his study of large companies that changed their identity and sense of direction, Hamel found that "more often than not it was not something that started at the top. It was started by people low down in the organization."[3]

REVERSE MENTORING

Most of us have had mentors that have been invaluable at some point in our career. My first mentor, while I was a young account executive at Young & Rubicam, was my boss Dick Nixon, who taught me the ropes on how to deal with a tough Proctor & Gamble client. Like most mentors, Dick was considerably older and more experienced.

But the world has changed. The over-forty crowd wants and needs to learn how to become adept in an environment that is fast becoming e-dominated. And an older and wiser mentor isn't going to do that for you. E-business mentors are the opposite of our old mentors. They are younger and less experienced in business but whizzes in a high-tech world.

Who better to teach you about high-tech stuff than someone who grew up with it? For many of us, learning computer skills was a struggle. But to someone in their twenties, it was a game that was fun, so they learned faster and easier.

Recognizing the wisdom of youth in these high-tech, e-everything days, GE has a program called reverse mentoring. Geek mentoring, as it is sometimes called, is a program in which one thousand Internet-savvy employees work closely with senior managers, one on one, to show them the ropes about using the Internet.

"What we did with this [program]," said GE chairman Jack Welch, "was tip the organization upside down so the senior people are all working with somebody junior."[4]

WARMING UP CUSTOMERS

At a session focusing on improving customer service at a major ski resort, one of the chairlift operators came up with the fabulous idea that I alluded to before. This eighteen-year-old young man, who had taken a semester off from college to ski, said, "People waiting on those long weekend lift lines are freezing. And to warm up, they have to trek all the way over to the ski lodge to get something hot to drink. It's a huge pain. It takes a lot of time and they have to take off their skis and clunk around the lodge in their ski boots. Why don't we take a snowmobile, get some tanks, fill them with coffee or hot cider, and sell it to people while they are on the lift line? That way they won't have to get out of line and take time from their skiing."

After the usual firehosing responses about what a mess the cups would make, management decided to give it a try. They had to refill the tanks eight times the first day! And it only got better after that. Expanding on the idea, they decided to set up small lift-line stands that sold other things as well, like energy bars and suntan lotion. These lift stalls worked so well that they were expanded to other lifts. This idea from a college kid taking the winter off to ski became not only a nifty little profit center for the ski resort but skyrocketed customer satisfaction levels and enhanced the resort's image as one that really cared about its guests.

COVERING YOUR PATIENT'S BUTT

One of the worst things about going to the hospital, aside from the needles, is the damn gown they give you. It only has one tie, which you can count on to come loose. The neck is so high it nearly strangles you, and the gown is so short it looks like a miniskirt that a teenybopper might hesitate to wear. It's also so skimpy that it usually only covers half your butt. To keep warm and cover up, many nurses actually encourage patients to put on two of them, one the right way and the other backwards.

Enter Mary Gonzalez, who had worked in maid services and the laundry room at Hillcrest Baptist Medical Center in Waco, Texas, for twenty-two years and had seen and heard every complaint. Finally figuring she could do better herself, she designed a new gown. On her own sewing machine she created one that was longer with more coverage, had a scoop neck for comfort, and three ties. And the wash-and-wear fabric she used is also slightly heavier, so her robe doesn't flap open every time someone sneezes. And get this, it was considerably cheaper than the old gown.

To make a long story short, the gown was an instant success. "They all wanted the gown," said Ed Hinkle, senior vice president of Volunteer Hospital of America's Southwest Division, speaking of his group of twenty-three hospitals. "They'll probably be showing this style in Paris before long," he joked.[5] Last I heard, they had sold over 250,000 of Mary's gowns.

CHECKING OUT

Many supermarkets are now open twenty-four hours a day in order to better serve their customers. One night a woman who was a manager at a high-tech firm was doing her shopping at her usual time—about ten P.M. Exhausted, she told

Clyde O'Brien, a high school dropout who worked the checkout counter on the late shift, that it would be great if she could get someone to do her shopping.

At the next staff meeting, Clyde told his manager the story and added, "I could do the shopping for her. Heck, there's usually no one in the store between midnight and six A.M. If I got a list, I could go around, fill her order, and we could have it ready for her in the morning or we could deliver it."

They tried the idea, telling shoppers that for a small charge they'd fill orders at night and have them either ready at the store or delivered to their house by eight A.M. They were swamped. It became such a profit center that they had to add extra "shoppers" to fill the orders at night. The service worked so well that the whole chain of over 150 stores started using it. Today, Clyde is a store manager.

WHO'S LISTENING?

Stories like this are everywhere. Christine Holton, a keynote speaker to women's groups, told me about a secretary for the American Dietetic Association who saved this nonprofit organization thousands of dollars. One of this young woman's tasks was to coordinate the many mailings that were sent regularly to their seventy-seven thousand volunteers. The problem was, she kept getting calls from volunteers who were complaining about receiving too many mailings and losing some of the single information sheets. Her solution was simple and obvious. Consolidate the many small mailings into one large one. Not only did her idea alleviate this source of volunteer complaints, it also significantly cut ADA's mailing costs.

When her manager congratulated and rewarded her for her initiative, the woman told her boss that she actually had the idea a while back, but had been reluctant to bring it up. Why? Because she was "just a secretary" and no one would listen.

A secretary, a high school dropout working the checkout register, a college student chairlift operator, a hospital laundry room employee—ideas are all around. Yet the response I always get when I ask people why they don't make more suggestions is universal: "No one listens."

Unfortunately, too many managers think they must have all the answers and solve all the problems themselves—that's what they are being paid for, after all—or so they think. This attitude prevents many executives from utilizing the creativity of their employees. As a result, old problems don't get solved and new opportunities don't develop.

Listening Aggressively

U.S. Navy captain Michael Abrashoff says the key is to listen aggressively. "Soon after arriving at my command, I realized that the young folks on my ship were smart and talented. My job was to pick up all of the ideas that they had for improving how we operate."[6]

The first step to being a good listener is to simply understand that your people are a great source for fresh ideas. The next step is to be open, interested, and to actively seek out ideas that may break the old rules or come from people far down the line. "Good listening is fueled by curiosity. It's hard to be a good listener if you aren't interested,"[7] says Ron Heifitz, the director of the leadership institute at Harvard's Kennedy School of Government and a best-selling author on leadership.

Listening Isn't a Skill, It's an Attitude

"Most leaders die with their mouths open," Heifitz continues. He then relates that the best leaders have always been dynamic listeners. "In the airline business, Jan Carlson at SAS in the early eighties, Colin Marshall at British Airways in the early nineties, and Herb Kelleher of Southwest are always encouraging ticket agents and baggage handlers to be creative.

[These leaders] are asking questions all the time and don't get seduced into trying to provide all the answers.

"If you're the boss, the people around you will invariably sit back and wait for you to speak," says Heifitz. "They will create a vacuum of silence, and you will feel a compelling need to fill it. You need to have a special discipline not to fill that vacuum."[8]

In his book *Clicks and Mortar*, David Pottruck, the co-CEO of financial giant Charles Schwab, discusses the importance of "listening to hear rather than listening to answer."[9] He says it is essential for managing the self-directed employees that information-age companies must have. "Listening is not so much a skill as it is an attitude with a single focus," says Pottruck.

Fred Andrews, the *New York Times* reviewer of the book, wrote about never having met Pottruck's equal as a listener in all his three decades of financial journalism. "The experience was like being bathed in respectful intelligent attention."[10]

We were all given the perfect equipment in the right proportion to be great listeners—two ears and one mouth. The problem is that these days, when speed is king and we're all in a hurry, most managers operate as if they had nine mouths and no ears. "Listen? Who's got time to listen? I've got to get this shipment out, prepare for this meeting, solve this problem!" is the refrain I hear time and again. One of the best ways to create exciting new opportunities, as well as to save yourself time and money and ultimately not have to work so damn hard, is to take the time to listen to your people. You literally can't afford not to.

UPLIFTING

Aside from being a great source for ideas and solutions, listening down is uplifting to your people. Showing you are interested in their ideas and opinions raises their morale, spirit, and confidence. Listening to someone shows you value their opinion and in turn increases their self-assurance. Very few people want to be bench sitters in life. Most people want to feel that they are making a contribution to the team and that they are valued.

It's important to realize that many people in starter jobs, especially those with little education in minimum wage positions, don't think of themselves as intelligent, which of course was probably driven into them in school. They have that "I'm just a secretary" or burger-flipper mentality, which results in a self-image that scrapes the floor and a work ethic of just going through the motions. Listening to them shows that you respect their opinion and that they are valued employees. This will help to elevate their self-image and self-confidence.

A self-confident, motivated employee is going to work harder, better serve the customer, and be an inspiration to others. These days, as it has become increasingly more difficult and expensive to recruit, motivate, and retain entry-level people, it is vitally important to have a person like this on your staff.

LISTENING ISN'T ENOUGH

Just listening, however, isn't enough. The biggest de-motivator for employees is to be told their ideas are important and then have nothing done with them. Lack of action or even a response to suggestions creates cynicism. Not acting or responding, after saying you're interested, is worse than never starting the process at all.

It's critical not just to listen, but to respond to your employees' ideas if you want to create an environment where people are more involved and motivated. That doesn't mean every idea has to be acted on. Some suggestions will not be viable, but you need to at least respond to these suggestions, even those you won't use.

Responding quickly to people's input and feedback shows respect and interest. It also improves the chances for getting breakthrough ideas. It may be a person's third idea that is the most worthy. But if you don't respond to the first, you'll never even get to the second.

"The rule at Southwest [Airlines] is if you get an idea, you read it quickly and respond instantaneously," says company founder Herb Kelleher, one of the most innovative and motivating leaders around. "You may say no, but you give a lot of reasons why you're saying no, or you may say we're going to experiment with it in the field, see if it works. But I think showing respect for people's ideas is very, very important because as soon as you stop doing that you stop getting ideas.

We tell people that if you need a suggestion box then you're not doing what you should be doing. You shouldn't have to interpose a box between you and the people with ideas. You ought to be with your people enough that they are comfortable to just pop on in and give you their ideas."[11]

Sure, it takes time to respond to ideas and suggestions. But it shows people that you care about them and are interested in their input. When people know you care about them, they'll care more about you and the job.

Listening down and responding will raise the level of motivation, innovation, and participation in your people. It will also help create a more enjoyable and exciting workplace for everyone. Getting good ideas from your people not only offers you more opportunities to break through to new levels, it also relieves the burden of having to come up with all the answers yourself. Ultimately, aggressively listening down and acting on what you hear will enable you to be far more successful than you thought you could be without working so damn hard.

➡ KEEP IN MIND

➡ Get a young mentor to teach high-tech skills.

➡ Respond to all ideas.

➡ Listen rather than talk.

➡ Ask questions rather than provide answers.

➡ Listening down raises people's confidence and motivation.

[1] *Fast Company,* June 1999, p. 150.

[2] Adam Bryant, "Like His Mentor at US Airways . . . ," *New York Times,* 27 September 2000, p. B6.

[3] Ibid.

[4] *Fortune,* 1 May 2000, p. 110.

[5] *Waco Tribune Herald,* 11 August 1997.

[6] *Fast Company,* June 1999, p. 150.

[7] Ibid.

[8] Ibid.

[9] *New York Times,* 30 April 2000, p. B7.

[10] Ibid.

[11] *Fortune,* 28 May 2001, p. 70.

CHAPTER 19

Odd Couples Make Perfect Partners

nthropologist Margaret Mead once said, "Never doubt that a small group of committed people can change the world."[1] Heeding this wisdom, American business is teeming with teams. With business becoming more complex and changing on a daily basis, the single-handed, do-it-yourself model of success no longer works.

Whether you are starting a new business or a new project, collaboration is essential. Teamwork, whether with a partner or a group, is a key to innovation and problem solving. To streamline operations, companies are sledgehammering the walls of the old silos and integrating new systems and people. Over three quarters of Fortune 1000 companies are using cross-functional teams.[2]

HOMOGENIZED TEAMS

One of the biggest obstacles to achieving results from teams is that people feel most comfortable working with like-minded individuals. The result is that teams often consist of people who think alike and who see the world or a problem through a similar lens. This will work if all you want to do is validate your viewpoint. If, however, you want to come up with revolutionary ideas, it's a big mistake to have a team consist of similar types of individuals.

177

Can you imagine a team made up of all salesmen, accountants, or lawyers? The salesmen would be focused on the top line, the accountants the bottom line, and the lawyers would be arguing. Though it may seem easier to have a team or partnership made up of people with similar perspectives, you'll rarely get imaginative results from a homogenized group.

DIVERSITY, DIFFERENCES, AND DISCOMFORT

Varying backgrounds and perspectives are the key to creative teams and partnerships. The more different points of view, the better your chances for coming up with unique ideas. "Great things happen when differences converge," writes futurist Joel Barker. "The intersection between differences is where most innovation occurs. When you increase diversity you increase your rate of innovation, and innovation is the most powerful way to stay competitive. Diversity is a crucial element for the health of any system. The best ideas will come from a wealth of points of view."[3]

I often asked groups whom they would rather have as a team member, a person who is on time or someone who is continually late? Someone who dresses in business attire or someone who has hair down their back, an earring, and wears a Grateful Dead T-shirt? Someone who is respectful and friendly and plays by the rules or someone who is abrupt, shocking, and keeps breaking rules? The group unanimously picked the former.

I then asked them who they thought would add a more creative element to their team. The answer was again unanimous. They all picked the opposite.

When asked where new ideas come from, Nicholas Negroponte, the head of MIT's Media Lab, said, "That's easy. From differences. Creativity comes from unlikely juxtapositions. The best way to maximize differences is to mix ages, cultures, and disciplines."[4]

SEEING THROUGH DIFFERENT EYES

Teams consisting of people from different parts of the globe will evoke the types of diverse views that are important for innovation. The reason for this, according to psychologist Dr. Richard Nisbett of the University of Michigan in his groundbreaking research comparing European Americans to East Asians, is that people who grow up in different cultures actually "think differently."[5]

In one study, Nisbett found that Japanese and American subjects viewed the same scene literally through different eyes. In an underwater scene in which a larger fish swam among smaller ones and other aquatic life, the Japanese focused on the context and relationships, whereas the Americans honed in on the content. The Japanese noted, for example, that "the big fish swam past the gray seaweed. Americans, on the other hand, were much more likely to zero in on the brightest object, the fish moving the fastest because that's where the money is as far as they are concerned," said Dr. Nisbett.[6]

In another study, when given a choice between two different types of philosophical arguments, Americans favored analytical logic devoted to resolving contradiction, whereas Japanese subjects favored a dialectical approach that accepts contradiction. Nisbett also found these same types of differences when they interpreted events in the social world.

"Don't choose a partner who is like you," says Robert Sullivan, the president of Information International. "A truly effective partner is someone with abilities and skills that complement your own and can expand what you can do as a team. If you're both engineers or have financial skills, for example, who will manage the sales and marketing?"[7]

In their magazine ads, investment banking giant Goldman Sachs focuses on the importance of diverse points of view for creative problem solving, telling us that "great minds don't think alike" and "the best ideas come from a room full of differing opinions."[8]

PLAYING THE RIGHT POSITION

Many entrepreneurs and managers make the mistake of trying to do it all by themselves. Oxford Health Systems founder Steven Wiggins is responsible for innovations that have changed managed health care for the better and set Oxford apart from rivals. But analysts blame him for misjudging the complexity and expense of a crippling computer system changeover and for losing control of the costs of medical claims. The result was that Oxford ended up losing $291 million and the stock plummeted.[9]

The problem was that Wiggins, like many entrepreneurs, was a great visionary but a lousy manager. "I'm an entrepreneur first, a professional manager second," he said.[10] But second doesn't cut it these days. You have to focus on what you do best.

Apple Computer got in trouble in its early days for the same reason. Steve Jobs was an inspired visionary, motivator, and product developer but lousy at managing a business. A primary reason that entrepreneurial people who start a business aren't good at managing it is because they have no passion for management.

Most entrepreneurs are innovators who love the excitement of starting something new and hate to have to sit at a desk and manage it. It's the same reason so many successful salespeople, designers, and engineers fail when they are promoted to management. They like the action and challenge of being in the trenches. A year after being promoted to a plum management spot, a design engineer for one of the major auto companies asked to go back to his old job. "All I was doing was pushing paper and managing people. I wasn't having any fun, which for me is the excitement of designing something new," he said.

Don Harris is the president and executive director of the Nehemiah Corporation, an innovative community development organization that gave out $155 million to forty-five thousand people for mortgage down payments on low-income housing in the last two years.

Speaking about his role, Harris, who founded Nehemiah in 1994, says, "I don't want to be the captain of the ship. I want to design the ship, not run it. I have partners and senior people to run it who do a much better job than I. My job is creating the next thing. I can't do that if I also have to keep the ship from crashing into the rocks, which"—he laughed—"is probably what would happen if I ran it."[11]

Put simply, some people are good starters and innovators, while others are good at running the operation once it gets going. Put either in the opposite job and they'll fail miserably. The perfect scenario is to have both people playing a position at which they can excel.

Odd Couples

No one is perfect. We all have holes in our game. The key to successful partnerships is to get people that complement each other's strengths and fill each other's gaps. The most successful teams are made up of opposites. Starters need finishers; bottom liners need top liners; idea people need detail people; passionate, fiery types need cool, rational ones for balance. Every visionary who is great at starting something and motivating people needs someone who is equally great at managing the organization once it gets off the ground.

One of the most innovative teams at Nissan Design International (the studio that has produced such trendsetting innovations as the Pathfinder sport utility vehicle, the Infiniti series, and the Mercury Villager minivan) is made up of Tom

Semple and Allan Flowers. Semple and Flowers have work styles that are as opposite as you can get. Semple starts a new design by clearing away all traces of earlier projects. He loves the freedom of a blank piece of paper. He rarely refers to engineering specs or marketing reports. He works on intuition. Flowers, on the other hand, "worries about nuts and bolts and conducts a methodical assessment of potential components and materials, of schedules and priorities."[12]

Jerry Hirschberg, Nissan Design's founder and president, believes in hiring divergent pairs. "When it comes to creativity, the best person for the job is often two people who see the world in utterly different ways."

Speaking of the pairing of Semple and Flowers, Hirschberg said, "Each approached a project with totally different priorities and work styles. The pairing was so successful that we said, 'Let's keep doing this.'"[13] Another of Hirschberg's successful teams is made up of a former eyeglass designer and a pure "car guy."

This pairing of opposites works best whether two people are starting a company or whether a group is starting a project or trying to solve a problem.

For instance, DoubleClick, one of the hottest companies in Silicon Alley, was founded by the odd-couple partnership of East Coaster Wenda Harris Millard, the street-smart former publisher of *Ad Weekly* and *Family Circle*, and Kevin O'Connor, a Midwesterner who ran software companies. "We come from totally different worlds," says Millard. "Sometimes we don't even speak the same language."[14]

Really Odd Couples

When attending auto shows and other events, Chris Bangle, design chief for BMW, pairs up members of his design team with engineers and finance people. The reason: "It helps the suits to understand what the designers are doing. Plus it's good for the designers to have a friend or two who sees why you must use leather that costs three times more than the budget call for."[15]

You can even pair up with your competitor. Mike Hammer, the originator of reengineering, calls this "virtual integration." "Imagine that you and I are competing yogurt manufacturers and that instead of sending our yogurt to stores on separate trucks, we decide to share a truck. It makes sense," he says. "We're not competing on the cost of trucking. We're competing on the flavor of the yogurt, on its freshness (and other specifics of the product and price) . . ."[16]

CREATIVE ABRASION OR HEAD KNOCKING?

Having differing points of view leads to what Nissan Design's Hirschberg calls "creative abrasion which produces wonderful creative sparks."[17] On the other hand, diverse perspectives, not handled properly, can also produce conflict, petty jealousies, and lack of flexibility. Look at what happened at Disney. Michael Eisner and Jeffrey Katzenberg were an innovative duo that had the Midas touch. Yet despite their immense talents, personality conflicts destroyed the relationship and cost Disney something around $100 million.

Many mergers suffer the same fate. When IBM, with its East Coast button-down culture, bought Rhome Communications, with its California-casual culture, their different perspectives could have made for great innovations. Unfortunately, the merger failed because each was convinced their way was best. They neglected to take the time to pool their strengths.

With all the mergers, consolidations, and acquisitions taking place today, this same pattern keeps recurring. Giant corporations that have merged in fields ranging from financial services to the oil industry are experiencing many casualties from the infighting that results from each group stuck in a "my way is better" mentality.

SYNERGISTIC SETTINGS

The setting is a key element to successful partnerships. If the mood is hostile, ego driven, and lacking in trust, nothing worthwhile will result. If the mood is open and trusting, great things can develop. Here are some rules for creating the type of environment where synergy can take place.

Get as many different points of view as possible. This includes people who know nothing about your field and therefore can supply that important "beginner's perspective." Plug the holes in your game with people with different strengths, interests, concerns, and backgrounds. Make sure all the bases—the necessary skills for solving a problem—are covered.

Conflict often leads to creativity. Cultivate disagreements. Use opposing points of view to create a larger perspective. Rather than trying to prove you are right, assume that both views are right. Creating a picture that can include both sides will often result in synergy and a breakthrough idea.

Target the idea, not the person. No personal attacks. Statements like "Leave it to a lawyer [or whoever] to come up with that," though delivered in jest, create defensiveness and hostility, which poison the environment and kill any chance for creativity, productivity, and teamwork.

Treat everyone with respect. Volume and rank don't necessarily produce the best solutions or the most innovative ideas. The introvert from R&D, the techie from the back room, or the shy receptionist can provide important perspectives and insights. Some of the best ideas come from the people and places you least expect. Make sure everyone has an opportunity to contribute.

Be open and consider everything. Don't dismiss anything; respect differences of opinion, beliefs, values, and ideas. The seeds of a brilliant idea may be contained in something that at first blush sounds crazy or is totally different from anything you had in mind.

Egos kill teamwork. If you feel that you or your idea has to win, more often than not you won't even consider what someone else has to offer. And if you win, that makes someone else a loser. Since no one wants to lose, this attitude creates defensiveness that inhibits creative problem solving and innovation.

Take a moment and think about your own strengths, interests, and concerns. Make a list of the holes in your game along with the things you hate doing. What types of competencies and people would you need on your team to help fill these holes? Don't forget that one of the most important rules for successful teamwork is to appreciate and cultivate differences.

))⟩➡ **KEEP IN MIND**

➡ Odd couples make the best partners; every starter needs a finisher.

➡ Creative abrasion leads to creative sparks.

➡ Uniformity of teams leads to conformity of ideas.

[1] Joey Reiman, *Thinking for a Living* (Marietta, Ga.: Longstreet, 1998), p. 30.

[2] *Fortune*, September 1994, p. 86.

[3] Ibid.

[4] Tom Peters, *Brand Everything Workbook*, 16 August 2000, p. 96.

[5] Erica Goode, "How Culture Molds Habits of Thought," *New York Times*, 8 August 2000, p. D1.

[6] Ibid.

[7] *Bottom Line*, January 2000.

[8] *Fortune*, 10 January 2000, Advertising section.

[9] *Business Week*, 9 March 1998, p. 38.

[10] Ibid.

[11] Don Harris, conversation with the author, 22 May 2000.

[12] *Fast Company*, December 1997/January 1998, p. 42.

[13] Ibid.

[14] Ibid.

[15] *Fast Company*, September 2001, p. 48.

[16] Ibid, p. 114.

[17] *Fast Company*, December 1997/January 1998, p. 42.

CHAPTER 20

Owning Your Customer

S everal years ago my finances were so scattered, I needed a bookkeeper to keep track of them," Bill W., a friend who had a successful consulting business, told me. "I owned three properties and each had a mortgage from a different bank. My mutual funds were handled by one person, stocks another, and my pension plan by a third. My business checking account was in one bank, my personal checking in another, and my credit cards were from others. I was working harder to keep track and manage my money than I did to make it.

"Now I have it all in one place," Bill continued. "My mortgages, business and personal checking accounts, credit cards, and investments are all handled by the same bank. The bonus is that I am a special customer for this bank and as a result get terrific care and service. I also have one person that I can call about any of my accounts. Does this cost me more? Just the opposite. I get a discount on my mortgages for being a special customer and don't have to fill out all of those annoying forms when I want to refinance or get another loan."

ONE-STOP SHOPPING

Bill's experience is reflective of what is transpiring in all kinds of businesses and industries today and will be even more so tomorrow. The trend if you are selling business-to-consumer (B2C) is one-stop shopping. If you are selling business-to-business (B2B), it's called single-source supplier. All types and sizes of business, especially those in industries that have been recently deregulated, are being redefined in order to take advantage of this trend.

The goal is to develop a relationship in which customers buy all of their needs from you. Or as the vice president of a megacorporation told me, the goal is to try to *own the customer.* In the financial services industries, companies are each seeking to handle all of your financial transactions, including loans, investments, checking accounts, and credit cards. This one-stop financial bazaar is also happening online. E*Trade is planning to add financial services that will rival anything on Wall Street. Chris Cotsakos, their CEO, says they will soon add online banking and loans and, through partners, sell insurance, mortgages, and even the ability to buy IPO stocks. "We'll be the one place you bookmark on your browser," vows Cotsakos.[1]

The same thing is happening in the telecommunications industry. Remember when AT&T was the phone company? Now this telecommunications giant, along with other corporations such as Sprint and MCI/WorldCom, are vying to handle all of your communication, information, and entertainment needs. In fact the headline for a *New York Times* article about how AT&T was branching out into all sorts of new businesses was "Ma Everything." Quite a switch from the old Ma Bell.[2] Utilities are also using their marketing power to sell you much more than just gas and electricity. Giants like Nevada's Sierra Pacific now offer everything from heat pumps to satellite dishes to kitchen ranges. They even have a mail-order catalogue business.

This one-stop trend is everywhere. Remember when your local supermarket just sold food? Now they peddle tools, tires, flowers, greeting cards, and garden equipment. Some even sell cars. You have drugstores with banks in them and banks selling drugs. You can even get great sandwiches at Wells Fargo's new location in San Francisco. Remember when stadiums used to be for watching a ball game and having a beer and a hot dog? Now the game is almost incidental. Ballparks have become a combination cruiseship and shopping mall.

Turning Airports into Air-Malls

Airports are a great example of one-stop shopping. One of the biggest problems for us "air warriors" arises when our flights are canceled, delayed, or rerouted. This happens with increasing frequency, and leaves us outraged at O'Hare, stranded in Seattle, or frantic in Philly.

But don't leap over the airline counter just yet. Airports have been reinvented to become business, entertainment, and shopping centers that take advantage of your "free" time. So after you're through pounding your PC, and your cell phone battery has run out, there's plenty to do at these "airmalls" besides hitting the bar or shopping in the understocked, overpriced stores that sell magazines, magnets, and Maalox.

You can brush up on your culture at San Francisco's United terminal, which has museum-quality exhibits, get a ten-minute neck massage to relieve your stress at the Dallas airport, or practice your putting at the Palm Springs airport. All airports have video games in which you can vent your anger on some evil alien, and Reno and Vegas have slots. Maybe you can't locate your luggage at Denver's new airport, but there's not much else you can't find there. Airports at Denver, Pittsburgh, and elsewhere are loaded with shops selling everything from toys to ties, books to boots, outerwear to underwear to software.

Because everyone these days has less time, this one-stop shopping works for the buyer as well as the seller. Anything that will save time and make our lives easier and less complicated, we're all for it. The key is convenience, and given our complex lives, everyone is looking for someone to make life simpler.

Single-Source Supplier

This trend toward one-stop shopping is occurring big-time in business-to-business transactions. Increasing numbers of companies are seeking single-source suppliers in many areas. Hewlett Packard, the $50 billion engineering and high-tech giant, previously had hundreds of vendors supplying them with personnel services. At last count they had six. Similarly, Ford Motors used to have numerous suppliers of blow-mold machines. They now have a contract with one company to make them all.

The reason for this trend is that everyone in the work-place is hassled with more to do in less time and overloaded with paperwork, e-mails, and meetings. Anything that will make life simpler and less complex is extremely appealing. Companies would rather have one supplier whom they know and trust than a whole carload. Sure, maybe by sending out a request for a bid, you can buy those widgets cheaper. But all the paperwork you have to do and the time it takes to deal with multiple suppliers costs you in time, money, stress, hassles, and headaches.

The president of one of the largest trucking companies switched from contracting with many tire dealers and service operations all over the country to having just one. He told me, "Previously I dealt with a whole slew of suppliers, which made it tough to get standardized service and quality. We were also getting a huge range of prices. Now I have one supplier, so whether our truck is in Washington, D.C., or Winache, Washington, I know what we are getting and how much it will cost. And I get one bill. It's great. It's much easier and actually in the long run cheaper."

Fat-Cat Shopping Mall

A business that has created one-stop shopping for a specific target market is the *duPont Registry*, started in 1985 by Tom duPont and two partners. The *Registry* is a very successful magazine that has no editorials or columns. It is simply a marketplace for people to buy or sell cars. But not ordinary, run-of-the-mill cars; the duPont Registry sells classic, exotic, and luxury rides.

Some of duPont's customers wanted to know if they could use the magazine to sell their boats. No, not rowboats with outboards, the big jobs—slick cabin cruisers and yachts. When opportunity knocks, duPont listens. So what comes next? Yep, you got it. *DuPont Registry* for boats. Then came the *duPont Registry* for homes, the kind we used to call mansions.

Tom duPont says he is called a plutographer, a follower of the affluent. "We're not looking for a million readers in these magazines. We're looking for readers with millions."

DuPont also has a Web page that provides the rich with information about the best places to eat and great vacations. He also now has an online auction site for luxury items. Not just for cars, boats, and homes, but anything exotic or classic, such as watches, antiques, jewelry, and artwork. DuPont says, "We want to be the eBay for the affluent. We're not looking for a million eyeballs, just eyeballs with millions."

By knowing his market, duPont has created what he calls a marketplace for the affluent, or what I call a fat-cat shopping mall, a one-stop shop for anyone with bucks.

The World's Worst Shopping Experience—No Longer

Buying a car used to be one of the all-time worst experiences. I always felt like I was walking into a shark feeding frenzy when I went into a car dealer. But Sergeant Insurance has taken the hassle out of buying a car. They started by identifying all of the steps involved in a purchase: researching, selecting, purchasing, financing, insuring, and servicing.

Sergeant will handle it all for you. Through partnerships they will find the selected car for you, negotiate the best purchase price, get the financing and insurance, and offer you a service package. And because they are doing this in volume, they can get you better prices than you would on your own.

Moving Nightmares

Another nightmare is everything you have to do when buying a new house and moving into it. But some aggressive Century 21 agents have made this a hassle-free experience. Partnering with various other suppliers of services, these agents not only find you a house, but get you a mortgage, pack you up, and move you. And when you arrive at your new home, they turn on your power, hook up your phone service, and even get you discounts from local retailers. They've turned a nightmare into a pleasant dream.

Like leaders in all businesses, these Century 21 brokers aren't sitting on their hands and resting on their laurels. "Staying ahead isn't just how fast we do transactions—it's about how fast we change the way we do business," says Ms. Marty Rodriguez, the top broker worldwide for Century 21, who for seven years has been first in the United States in both unit sales and gross commissions.

"We were one of the first brokerages . . . to offer a full range of services on-site. We have our own escrow company and our own mortgage company. When buyers come in, we can get them prequalified on the spot, and we can write up a mortgage immediately after closing the deal. Now we're asking, how can we use our relationships with banks and other lending institutions to create even better service?"[3]

A Gas of an Auto Dealer

Theme parks, theme restaurants, theme stores . . . been there, done that, you say. But how about a one-stop theme auto dealership? The Armory Automotive Family Center is a glitzy two-story atrium that features a giant spark plug and fan belt on the ceiling and vintage gas pumps all around. At Armory you can gas up, get a lube job, and have your car washed, as well as get a burger and a manicure. It's a place to shop for a car, listen to jazz, shoot pool, and just hang out. You can also buy car kitsch like Grand Prix clocks and NASCAR sneakers.

Donald Metzner, Armory's president, conceived of the idea as a way to draw and preserve customers. His idea was for service and car wash customers to have a place to be entertained and spend money. "We're doing everything we can to bring the customer back as often as possible," says Metzner.[4] His idea seems to be working. He estimates that more than one thousand people a day come to the center, and sales of his dealership are up 30 percent.

No More Service Contracts

You probably have a drawer full of service contracts for everything from your washer and dryer to your air conditioners. Well, chuck them all out. Farmers Insurance and Sears Home Administrative Services offer you a single-source expanded home protection insurance product that covers appliances, heating and cooling systems, and plumbing and electric systems. This policy, according to the *Property Insurance Report*, "saves customers the inconvenience of finding quality technicians to service their appliances and it saves them money by limiting out-of-pocket expenses. It also provides better reliability and accountability than typical home warranty programs."[5]

No-Stop Shopping

How much time do you spend each week shopping for food and running miscellaneous errands? Probably three or four hours that you don't have. Well, Tim DeMello founded Streamline to make those shopping trips a thing of the past. Streamline offers customized home delivery of different products and services, including groceries, pharmaceuticals, office supplies, photo processing, laundry and dry cleaning, and rental videotapes. Too tired to cook? Streamline offers fully prepared meals.

For a forty-nine-dollar setup fee and thirty dollars a month (isn't your time worth more than that?), Streamline delivers items on your list and picks up other things, such as videotapes to be returned or laundry or dry cleaning to be done. And you can update your shopping list whenever you like.

DeMello is constantly on the prowl for additional items to be delivered. Based on wishes from his customers, he is now considering things like flowers and shoe repair.[6] You may never have to leave your house with this no-stop shopping service.

Nordstroms of the Corporate World

The legal arena was tough enough when law firms had only other law firms as competitors. But an ominous competitor has entered the game—the Big Five accounting firms, such as Arthur Andersen, Deloitte & Touche, and PricewaterhouseCoopers, whose revenues exceeded $40 billion last year and who employ more than 450,000 people. These giants are now fashioning themselves as a kind of Nordstroms of the corporate world. Clients of these professional service firms can get it all from them: accounting and tax services, consulting, change management, and information technology.

Recognizing that their clients are outsourcing as much as possible and want a single source to deal with, the Big Five have now expanded their one-stop offering to legal services. Illustrating the value to the client of this new service, former Pillsbury, Madison & Sutro litigator John Cadarette, who recently took a post at Arthur Andersen, said, "This firm allows me to bring in an expert in any discipline from anywhere in the world. A law firm might have a network of other lawyers to help your clients, but it is usually limited to legal work. Here, we are always looking to help a client in its business performance."[7]

Lawyers Fight Back

Law firms are also getting into the one-stop game. A growing number are turning to nonlegal businesses in order to serve their clients as well as improve their bottom line. Boston-based Bingham Dana, for instance, now offers a consulting service that develops state-by-state strategies for companies in highly regulated businesses and a strategic advising company that helps small to midsize companies with mergers and acquisitions, joint ventures, as well as access to venture capital.

Jay S. Zimmerman, Bingham's managing partner, said that the "big accounting firms took their two main assets, reputation and client base, and leveraged them by effectively cross-selling, creating a whole line of businesses which became very lucrative. Law firms have the same assets and can likewise provide a combined integrated approach."[8] For example, when John Harrington, the CEO of the Boston Red Sox, which had used Bingham Dana lawyers for over seventy years, decided to sell the team he turned to the firm's newly created strategic advice unit to handle the deal.

"These law firms are the latest evolution in a legal market which has transformed law firms from a small collection of general practitioners to highly specialized and global megafirms"[9] writes *New York Times* reporter Crystal Nix Hines. Many firms now offer a broad array of businesses, which include environmental consulting, human resource outsourcing, real estate title searching, and money management.

MAKING YOUR STOP THE ONE

When thinking about how to turn your business into the one stop your customer will make, ask yourself how you might be able to make your customer's life easier by adding something that would not only represent extra value, but save them time, money, and hassles. And what else would be more convenient for your customer to purchase from you that they now buy from someone else?

A young man who owned a car wash did this exercise. Noticing that his customers were standing around for ten to fifteen minutes while their car was being washed, he set up a little stand that sold cappuccino and bagels. That was so successful that he opened a convenience store. Realizing that the people were there for their cars, he put in a few pumps and a store that sold parts and accessories. He then called it a "Human Service Station" and now owns ten of them.

On a megalevel there is the ad where a Sony executive wakes up and says, "Hey, what are we? We're just a big factory for digitizing stuff. It happens that all these years we've been digitizing music. But ... if we can digitize anything, why don't we digitize baby pictures, too? Why don't we be *Sony and Kodak*. With our digital camera you can take pictures, store and edit them on your computer, and then print them. And then someone in shipping says, 'Hey, while we are digitizing these baby pictures we could also be e-mailing them around the world.' Because once they are digitized ... our customers can then send them on modems to grandparents on other continents. So we can be *Sony, Kodak, and Federal Express* all at the same time."[10]

Don't Go It Alone

Creating a one-stop shop or becoming a single-source supplier can be done in either of two ways. You can buy the resources yourself, like the Big Five accounting firms that hired their own lawyers or the gas station owner that bought a Starbucks franchise. Or you can adopt the strategy that most companies seem to be taking, which is to partner or form an affiliation with others in order to offer a more complete one-stop or single-source service. By partnering with other resources, E*Trade wants to be your financial bookmark, just as Charles Schwab now wants to be "the consolidator, the integrator ... for all of the pockets of your financial life."[11] Schwab arranged with investment banks Credit Suisse First Boston and Hambrecht & Quist to offer Wall Street stock research. They are also teaming up with the search engine Excite and Intuit's quicken.com to share content about retirement, investing, mortgages, taxes, and insurance.[12]

But unlike Schwab, you don't have to be a giant to find a partner. Teaming up is a way that little guys can offer one-stop shopping to their clients.

Remember, you don't have to go it alone. Find a partner who offers something that complements your own business. By making your customers' lives easier, your shop can be the one stop that they make.

➤ **KEEP IN MIND:**
- ➤ Most customers would rather make one stop than many.
- ➤ Most clients would rather have one source than many.
- ➤ Don't let old definitions limit new possibilities.
- ➤ Partner, merge, and consolidate in order to broaden your business.

[1] *Business Week*, 27 September 1999, p. 34.

[2] Thomas L. Friedman. *The Lexus and the Olive Tree*. (New York: Anchor Books, 2000), p. 85.

[3] *Fast Company*, February/March 1999, p. 52.

[4] *San Francisco Chronicle*, 31 September 1999, p. C5.

[5] *Property Insurance Report*, 22 March 1999, p. 3.

[6] *International Mass Retail Association*, 1999, p. 9.

[7] Ibid.

[8] *New York Times*, 31 May 2001, p. C1.

[9] Ibid.

[10] Thomas L. Friedman. *The Lexus and the Olive Tree*, (New York: Anchor Books, 2000), p. 83.

[11] *Fortune*, 7 December 1998, p. 100.

[12] Ibid.

CHAPTER 21

Doing the Impossible for Your Customer

Want a great source for inspired ideas? "Hey, it's easy," I'm told, "just ask the customer." But getting reliable feedback from your customer is trickier than you think. Many of the most frequently used tactics for getting this type of information aren't worth a damn.

QUERULOUS QUESTIONNAIRES

Did you ever get asked to complete a questionnaire by a hotel? Ever fill one out? Less than 20 percent of all people do. And those who respond usually do so because they are angry that their room service was delayed or the wake-up call failed to happen. While these forms may help hotel management become aware of a potential problem, the information usually isn't applicable because it reflects the thinking of such a small percentage of people.

Another problem with these questionnaires is that they are usually multiple choice. This doesn't leave room for the customer to elaborate and, therefore, doesn't provide the researcher with meaningful information. Sure, there is space for "additional comments," but the space is so limited that all you get is a one-line response that is usually too terse to give you much valuable information. And if you only get about a 20 percent response to the questionnaires, what percentage of those will take the time (which no one has enough of) to fill out the additional-comments section? So forget question-naires. They're a waste of money, paper, trees, and everyone's valuable time.

FOGGY FOCUS GROUPS

"It's important to get the voice of customers, to capture their words, in order to really understand what they want," the head of a major training company told me. Makes sense. But it ain't so easy to get the real skinny from them. Take focus groups, which are often seen as the answer for learning what the customer really wants. They're certainly better than the Q&A surveys in terms of giving you a richer and more reliable tapestry of information. They're also relatively inexpensive and pretty easy to administer.

But a panacea they're not. There are numerous problems with these groups. First of all, you have to conduct a large number of them in order to get a statistically significant sample. You also have to be sure that the groups are representative of your customers, although that's not the real problem. Even if you get a large and reliable sample, they are prone to bias.

Remember the classic film *Twelve Angry Men*, in which one persuasive character played by Henry Fonda brought the others around to his point of view? I have seen the same thing happen in many focus groups. One very articulate or powerful person influences the others. Shy or introverted people may be too intimidated to speak if their opinion runs counter to the rest of the group. Others may not tell you how they really feel or think for fear of sounding stupid, politically incorrect, or socially unacceptable.

DON'T BE CUSTOMER LED

Another pitfall of simply "asking the customer," says Douglas Atkin, the director of strategic planning at New York ad agency Merkley Newman Harty, is that "these days you can't succeed as a company if you're consumer-led, because in a world full of so much constant change, consumers can't anticipate the next big thing."[1]

The problem with asking your customers what they want is that they will usually request what they think is realistic and possible. After a speech I gave to the Association of Automotive Engineers, the head of engineering for Caterpillar Tractor told me, "If you had asked a farmer at the turn of the last century what he really wanted, the response probably would have been 'two horses that are bigger and stronger so they can pull my plow faster and longer.' He wouldn't have asked for a tractor."

Why not? *Hadn't been invented.*

A while back, how many manufacturers would have requested that a freight carrier deliver their shipments to the customer absolutely, positively by ten-thirty the next morning? None?

Why not? *Never been done before.*

Who would have asked for a machine in which you could insert a document that the recipient would receive almost instantaneously? Or in the days of carbon paper, who would have asked for a machine that would instantaneously copy a piece of paper in color and collate it at the same time? And how many homemakers would have said they wanted an oven in which they could cook their whole meal in five minutes?

Why not? Impossible, they thought.

No customer would have asked for a fax, a microwave oven, a Xerox copier, FedEx, or a hundred other breakthroughs. Why? Because they hadn't been invented, had never been done, or were thought to be impossible.

When asked what we want, most of us will respond with a request that we think is in the realm of possibility or a logical extension of the present. Something that is achievable and believable that we have experienced or at least heard or read about. We don't want to sound like a kid asking for something too far out of the realm of possibility. And we don't want to risk sounding stupid or unreasonable by asking for something we won't get. So we stick to what we think is possible, something maybe a little faster or stronger.

FUTURE THINK

"One of the reasons the popular prognosticators of the past never got it right is because they tended to envision our lives as filled with the same things as they already had, only better," writes *New York Times* columnist Gail Collins. "They didn't conceive of computers or faxes; they thought about pneumatic tubes going really, really fast."

Imagining life in the twenty-first century, Collins continues, "They predicted something approaching radio. . . . We're pictured listening to a news broadcast on what looks like a Victrola attached to a small electric power plant. But they never figured out television, possibly because they couldn't stretch their minds around what having a perpetual entertainment machine in every living room would do to family life."[2]

This same type of logical-extension thinking gets you to reengineer what you already have rather than reconceive it, re-create it, or invent it.

CONSIDER THE IMPOSSIBLE

Rather than following your customer, you want to lead them to places they've never been or deemed possible. You need to fuel their imagination, to get them to think outside the reality box. Have them thinking about what would be *ideal* rather than about what is *real*. Encourage them to consider the unrealistic and impossible. Pull from them ideas that they haven't thought about because they don't seem practical or doable. Remember, *what can't be done and hasn't been invented today will most certainly happen by tomorrow.*

One way to get people out of their rational, logical, practical mind-set is to have them complain (we're all good at that) about what isn't working and what is their biggest headache. The next step is to transform the complaint into something that would be ideal. Here are a couple of scripts:

- "My biggest headache is . . . It'd be great if you could . . ."
- "I know it's impossible (sounds crazy, unrealistic, impractical) but what I'd really love is . . ."
- "I know it's never been done, but what if you could . . ."
- "I'd give you all of my business (shop in your store all the time) if only you would . . ."
- "If I were king (or queen) of the world, I'd have you . . ."
- "What I really hate is . . . *What if* you could . . ."

Showing Up, Not Picking Up

Automobile dealers are going out of their way to provide great services these days. Many will pick up your car when it needs servicing. Some will even give you a loaner to use while your car is in the shop. But Toyota is always trying to do what was previously considered impossible in terms of customer service. Lexus, Toyota's premier line, gathers information by having loyal customers talk about what they like and, more importantly, what they dislike.

Lexus has fewer than two hundred dealers in the United States, so it's a major annoyance for customers needing routine service to have to take the car back to the original dealer, which is sometimes hundreds of miles away. To overcome that headache, Tony Fujita, Lexus vice president of Parts, Service, and Customer Satisfaction, says, "We've begun a new service.

We've converted a truck into a mobile service station that we can roll into a customer's driveway."[3]

No Shopping

At a "stretch the customer's imagination" session for a large supermarket chain in the Southwest, a single mother responded in a sarcastic vein, saying, "My biggest headache? It's having to go into your store. I'm so busy at the office that I often don't get home till seven. Then I have to get dinner for the kids and help them with homework. On the weekends, I am busy with everything from soccer games to sleepovers. Who's got time to shop? What would be really great is if I could have somebody do my shopping for me."

Out of that conversation came the idea to offer people the possibility to have their credit card on file and be able to call in an order. Some people even began faxing and e-mailing orders from the office and picking them up on their way home from work.

No Waiting

In a similar session I conducted for a quick-lube business, a bank manager responded by saying, "It's such a pain to go to your shop, which is across town and takes me out of my way. Then I have to wait for the car to be serviced and drive back to work. I lose almost an hour and I can't afford that. You know what would be great? Since I don't use my car at work, it would be terrific if you would pick it up from the garage, lube it, fill it up with gas, and maybe even wash it and leave it sitting there at the end of the day all ready to go. If you did that, I could get you lots of business."

Bingo! That quick-lube outlet took the bank manager's suggestion to heart. It now has gas pumps and a car wash on its facility. And most of its work is done by picking up cars from downtown. They charge extra for the service, but no one seems to mind.

From 135 to 1

"My biggest headache," the vice president of human resources for a multibillion-dollar manufacturing company said, "is that I have 135 personnel recruiters across the country to deal with. That means 135 contracts, 135 invoices, 135 communications, and e-mails up the gazoo. Ugh, I'd give anything to have one resource to do it all."

And one of the largest recruiters did just that. By creating partnerships and outsourcing with other recruiters, executive search companies, and even temp agencies, they became the point company for all of that human resource director's recruiting needs.

Road Warrior's Dream

Speaking of complaints, I have a big one. What really gets me at the end of a long, exhausting day of traveling is waiting on line at the check-in counter at the hotel. It may only be ten minutes, but it seems like a hundred after a day of traveling. And who wants to wait ten more minutes, regardless of the situation?

Taking it to the next step, *wouldn't it be great if* . . . you could just put your credit card in an ATM-type slot, punch a few buttons, and get your room key? Or, like the rental car counter, the hotel could have your folder and key ready so you could just pick it up and go to your room?

In this high-tech world, I am sure hotels can do something so that people who have reservations don't have to wait on line. Most of us belong to their frequent-bed or whatever-it's-called program anyway, so they have all our information.

Flying to the Rescue

Another way to come up with a bold idea is to put yourself in your customers' shoes and imagine doing something thought to be impossible to solve one of their problems. Hartness International is a twenty-six-year-old firm that manufactures high-speed machines that load bottles of soda, syrup, or ketchup into cartons for shipping. Dull, boring, not so sexy. Uh-uh. We can all learn about solving customer service problems from this Greenville, South Carolina, company.

Problems with case-packing machines in the bottling industry can bring an entire production line to a halt, costing a bottler as much as $150 *per minute*. So if the technician arrives and fixes the problem in a day—considered good service in that industry—the bottler has still lost $216,000!

Realizing this problem, Hartness's first innovation when they started the company in 1974 was—are you ready for this?—to hire only service technicians that were also *licensed pilots*. Got a problem? A tech pilot would fly to the rescue in one of the company's four planes, so the technician wouldn't have to wait around at an airport for the next flight.

But that was yesterday. Hartness is a model for changing times, a company that is not satisfied with something just because it works. They are constantly seeking the next step and are always looking to add new dimensions to their game. In this case the next step was, "How can we get to the customer *the moment* they need us? Airplanes aren't fast enough anymore," said Hartness CEO Bern McPheely.[4]

McPheely's next question was, "What if we could see the machines?"[5] (Asking "what if" is a great way to stimulate out-of-the-box thinking).

The technology for doing that didn't exist, so Hartness created it. With the Video Response System they developed, Hartness's engineers can now conduct live, interactive repairs immediately after a malfunction arises. The company estimates it can handle up to 80 percent of its service calls with a short video exchange. So forget same-day service. Hartness's customers now can get same-hour service.

Not satisfied with merely solving the customers' problems quickly, Hartness is now on to the next step, which is to help the customer solve their own problems. Every Hartness VRS Intervention is in effect a coaching session that teaches the client more about the equipment. The system also stores a video record of the session, so that if the problem happens again, the customer can solve it without Hartness's help. "That's the ultimate form of service," McPheely says.[6]

By doing the impossible, Hartness today has five thousand customers in ninety countries.

))))➧ KEEP IN MIND

- ➧ Lead your customer.
- ➧ Stretch your clients' imaginations to think beyond what is possible.
- ➧ Don't satisfy customers, surprise and amaze them.
- ➧ Today's impossibilities are tomorrow's opportunities.

[1] *Fast Company*, April 2000, p. 82.
[2] *New York Times*, 7 December 1999, p. A31.
[3] *Fast Company*, March 2000, p. 118.
[4] *Fast Company*, February/March 1998, p. 34
[5] Ibid.
[6] Ibid.

CHAPTER 22

Bulking Up the Little Guys

THE E-LANCE ECONOMY

Everywhere you look, small businesses, including the mom-and-pops that were once the heart of American business, are being steamrolled by national chains. With all the mergers, consolidations, and acquisitions taking place these days, it's easy to speculate that not too far in the future everything will be run by Disney, Citicorp, AOL, and the mega-oil conglomerate.

Dr. Thomas Malone, a professor at MIT's Sloan School of Management, and an alumnus of Xerox's creative Palo Alto Research Center, thinks differently. Malone has coined the term "e-lance economy" (a play on the word "freelance"). He envisions, "A business landscape in which much of the work that large businesses now do will be done instead by temporary companies—ad hoc combinations of small specialist firms that come together to tackle a single project and disband after its completion."[1]

Malone's view is that the new century will bring a "new golden age for small enterprise and a springtime for individual creativity in business. Communications in the Internet era will be so powerful, so rich, so cheap that even the smallest enterprises, already nimble, will be armed with the information they need to compete with corporate giants."[2]

DON'T TRY TO OUTPRICE THEM

One major mistake the "Davids" of the business world make is trying to compete directly with the Goliaths by lowering prices. This is one battle the little guys will always lose. Because of their size, the big guys can buy in huge quantities and pay less for their products. Therefore, they can afford to offer lower prices and still make a profit. Having deeper pockets, the Blockbusters, Home and Office Depots, Wal-Marts and Costcos of the world can also afford to do more promotion. And if they lose money for a few months, no big deal, because in the process they also eliminate the competition.

The airline industry is a great example of this scenario. A small airline opens up offering terrific prices for a few specific routes. The big guys feel threatened and counter by offering flights to those same destinations for lower fares even though they will now lose money on that route. Because the public is price conscious, they will of course go for the cheaper seats, and in a few months the start-up will have crashed and burned. And guess what? The big guy will immediately raise his prices.

QUICK STARTERS

Despite this disturbing trend small retailers are thriving by reinventing themselves. The advantages that small businesses have over large companies are speed and innovation. Once they come up with an idea, they can quickly put it into action. The giants, on the other hand, usually move with all the speed of plodding Goliaths. Getting a new idea approved in a big company usually means sending it up the line, and more often than not encountering a lot of firehosing from people who haven't talked to a customer in years.

One reason I love working with entrepreneurs is that when they like an idea, they take off and run with it. After conducting a program at the annual convention for the National Association of Landscape Contractors, I received a letter from the owner of a small contracting business in Northern California, who told me he acted upon my idea about expanding the game and opened up a nursery to sell to retail customers as well as other contractors. He has also started planning a landscape mall and already signed up a flower shop, a garden shop, a firm of landscape architects, and a swimming pool manufacturer. Additionally, he now distributes a newsletter with gardening and landscaping tips to all his customers. What's most amazing is that all of this has happened in the span of less than *three months*.

PERSONALIZE SERVICE

Many megastores with an operational focus on keeping lean— this often translates to mean—suffer from having an impersonal staff that is stretched thin by having to do more with less. Small companies can thrive by offering services that larger companies aren't equipped to provide. They are in a better position to give personal service and create a warm environment.

One supermarket in a suburb of San Francisco that had been overrun by the big chains did just that. Knowing most of their clientele had little time to shop, the market, like many others today, would, in addition to delivering orders that were phoned, faxed, or e-mailed in, pick up your dry cleaning, a video, and even some take-out. No big deal, you might think. Well, have you ever seen Safeway do that?

But then this little market started to really expand their game. They opened a gourmet wine-and-cheese section that featured a monthly wine and cheese tasting, a wine-of-the-month special, and a newsletter announcing these events. The owner told me he realized he had to start offering more personal services and create a caring environment in order to remain successful and profitable. His approach worked so well that he recently opened up similar stores in two neighboring towns.

Jane W., the owner of a small pet shop, realized she had better do something special in order to compete with the Pet Smart and Petco that had opened in malls near her. In the face of this hostile environment, she actually expanded her business by offering services like obedience training, grooming classes, counseling on how to pick the right pet, and boarding pets when owners were out of town. Needless to say, business soon picked up.

FIND A SMALL NICHE

After learning that her infant son's health problems were being caused by a chemical in standard-brand laundry detergents, Amilya Antonetti figured other parents might be experiencing the same problem. She went on to develop a line of hypoallergenic cleansers. But when she went to sell them to the supermarkets, she was laughed at. "Ever hear of Clorox or Tide? There's no place for you here," the store manager said.

After doing extensive promotion targeted to mothers for five years, she is no longer being laughed at by grocery stores. Amilya Antonetti's Soapworks line has shelf space in 2,500 stores nationwide and sales have exceeded $5 million. "There was clearly a niche that wasn't being served," Antonetti said.[3]

There are many potentially profitable small niches that the big guys don't want to bother with that merchants like Antonetti are very happy to.

CREATE COMMUNITY

The story line from the movie *You've Got Mail* centers on a big national bookstore chain running an independent store out of business. Unfortunately, this is not a fairy tale. In the early seventies independent stores were pretty much the backbone of the book market. But by 1991, given the competition from giants like Borders, Barnes & Noble, and Wal-Mart, sales by independents represented only 30 percent of the market for adult trade books and shrank even further to 18 percent in 1996.[4] But many independent bookstores are not only surviving but thriving by changing their sales and marketing strategies.

Politics and Prose, a small bookstore in Baltimore, succeeds by creating community. A monthly newsletter notifies neighbors of upcoming events and provides book reviews written by the staff. The store also launched its own book club, hosting monthly meetings for a number of different genres—today there are a total of thirteen. They also sponsor appearances and readings by local authors, which as many as 350 people attend. To foster the feeling of community, the store has opened a café. They also coordinate off-site events by making presentations at local schools and community centers.

This inclusive approach has paid dividends. Sales have gone up significantly over the last few years. "A corporate store can't replicate what we have. Without that spirit inside, it's an empty shell," says Politics and Prose owner Carla Cohen.[5]

Both large and small bookstores are offering speakers' series as a way of getting readers into the store. Independent bookseller Warren Cassell, of Greenwich, Connecticut, has taken this one step further. He arranges for authors to speak at local schools and clubs. He had Sebastian Junger, author of the best-seller *The Perfect Storm*, speak at both Brunswick Academy and Greenwich Academy as well as to two hundred adults at the nearby Indian Harbor Yacht Club. His quid pro quo was to have presold each of those five hundred students a copy of the book as enrichment reading. That's not all: Cassell also arranged to supply the schools with speakers and books on a continuing basis. Everybody wins—the school gets top-of-the-line authors for free and Cassell sells five hundred books.

Maureen Egen, the president of Time Warner's trade publishing operation, says that what Mr. Cassell and thriving independent retailers like him have succeeded in doing brilliantly is "to take the store to the public and cater to their tastes and interests."[6] Though Ms. Egen's statement referred to booksellers, she could have been talking about any type of small retailer regardless of the product they sell.

EXPAND THE WALLS

A small business can reinvent itself by reaching out. Prior to a speech I gave at a major convention in Philadelphia, the owner of a local bookstore called and asked if I would stay and autograph books after my speech. I signed over 250 books that day and he eventually sold every copy. "I do this at every convention and major conference that comes here," he told me. "It was a lot of work to get started. I had to make contacts with the Convention and Visitors Bureau and hotels to get a list of the meetings. Then I called the speakers who had written books to see if they were willing to stay and do a signing.

"It's something that no big store has done and it's turned out really great. The sponsor of the meeting gets to offer the books without having to lay out any money. People who like the speaker's message get to buy the book and get it autographed, which they love. And I don't have to do any special promotion or marketing. I just show up with a pile of books. And I can return any I don't sell to the publisher. It's great. You know how long it would take me to sell 250 books in my store," he said, smiling.

This enterprising bookstore owner also told me that he had become the bookstore for several national associations that were based in the city. "We publish a small catalogue of related books for each group, which they mail to the members. We then process the orders and ship them out and give the association a percentage of sales."

COOL, NOT BIG

One way for a small company to succeed in a big market is by being cool. Robert Earl Wells, often called the Martha Stewart of the youth culture, helped Jones Soda Co. of Vancouver break into the supercompetitive American beverage market in 1996. He introduced a "killer cool" blue bubble gum flavor that, according to Wells, "seemed happening and something the kids would definitely want to drink."[7]

To spread the word, Wells had Jones deploy a sales staff that left coolers full of soda at all the local surf shops and plastered ads at skateboard competitions and parks. "You can't get any cooler than that," says Wells.[8]

"The best was when the big guys, Coke and Pepsi, started using tactics we were using, like sending hot chicks to the same shops with arms full of coolers. That's cool," says Wells. "That means that you're getting noticed by the competition and you must be doing something right." But the shops said, "No way." They only wanted Jones—the smaller guy.[9]

Wells also had Jones give some of its proceeds to LIFEBEAT, the music industry charity that supports AIDS research and prevention. "All of a sudden Jones Soda was this little company that supported action sports and music. Now some of the most well-known athletes, like skateboarder Tony Hawk and biker Mat Hoffman, pass out Jones's bottles during these events." The lesson, according to Wells, is that "you don't need to spend all that much money to get the message out to compete with the big guys."[10]

ACT BIG

Imagine how tough it must be for local hardware stores to survive, much less succeed, faced with competitors like Home Depot and Lowe's. But Alex Rech, also known as Dr. Hardware, who is the founder of family-run Parkway Hardware in Westchester, Pennsylvania, has found a way. He and his daughter, an expert in all types of hardware and home improvement, started a local radio show called "Hardware Talk" that features "nuts and bolts" discussions on everything from carpentry and woodworking to fireplaces and woodstoves.

The show was so successful that this dynamic duo of home do-it-yourselfers opened a Parkway Hardware Web site and began broadcasting "Hardware Talk" live over the Internet. Listeners tune in regularly from as far away as Thailand and South America. They now have customers from all over the world who not only order from their Web site but make annual pilgrimages to their store.

"The Web absolutely gives us a surge in business," Ms. Rech Binder said. "We are competing with Home Depot and Lowe's, and because of the Internet we are doing just fine. I was pretty nervous when those stores opened near us, but it really hasn't affected us at all."[11]

ADDING CLICKS TO BRICKS

Scott Matthews, the founder of a Web development company called Turnstyle.com, says, "The Internet is the new fax machine. It's just another way to help small business operators deepen their relationship with customers and extend their businesses."[12]

A survey by the National Trust for Historic Preservation found that small merchants that sell online have experienced a 12.8 percent growth in overall sales and that 14.3 percent of their sales were now attributed to the Internet. And keep in mind that for a small operation, even a 5 percent increase in sales can mean the difference between surviving and closing down.[13]

The study found that these small retailers do best on the Internet by focusing on unusual products or excellent, personalized service. A good example is Buch Spieler, a music shop in Montpelier, Vermont, that sells out-of-print movie soundtracks and other offbeat items. This little store off the beaten path experienced a 10 percent growth in sales and a 20 percent increase in customer base since they went online.[14]

David Cullen, a vice president of the National Federation of Independent Businesses in Washington, said he couldn't think of a business that wouldn't benefit from being online. "Main Street entrepreneurs could get their second winds by using the Internet," says Mr. Cullen. "Imagine a local quick oil change shop that sends e-mails to its clients when it is time for an oil change. . . . Their customers feel like they have more direct communication with the shop."[15]

The technology is now available for even the smallest mom-and-pop shops to go global using the Internet. This means that a local Boston widget manufacturer can sell products to customers in Belize and Bombay just as easily as he can to those in Braintree.

GET HELP—OUTSOURCE

Outsourcing can help small companies compete by allowing them to offer more services and products. "Outsourcing levels the playing field," says Frank Casale, the executive director of the Outsourcing Institute. "Outsourcing enables a small business to bring anything to market and compete with the largest organization in the world," continues Casale. He tells a story about a regional florist who feared he wouldn't be able to expand because his fleet of trucks was too small. In the old days the company would have probably bought or leased more trucks and then recruited and trained the drivers to solve this problem. Now they outsource the shipping to a company that already has the resources and expertise. Just like that they became a national company.

The Topsy Tail Co., with three employees, started by selling a nylon wand used to style hair, which went on to become a huge success. By hiring outside firms to handle manufacturing, accounting, advertising, and shipping, Topsy Tail did $80 million in sales the year after they opened for business, without adding a single employee.

These days many small companies are outsourcing their main business software for managing areas such as accounting, manufacturing, sales management, human resources, and travel. This relationship with an applications service provider (ASP) saves the expense of hiring a computing staff. Pat Golden, the CFO of Rave Sports, a small, privately held maker of inflatable trampolines, says that having an ASP run their computer operations "has helped them eliminate having to spend a lot of cash upfront."[16]

SPIN IT DIFFERENTLY

You can gain a competitive advantage by creating a product with different spin and appeal. In the 1950s and 60s everyone was driving big Detroit gas-guzzling monsters, bedecked with fins, duals, and gigando V8 motors. Then VW came out with the "bug," which revolutionized the auto industry with little more than a sewing machine for an engine and a heater about the size of your toaster. Volkswagen didn't compete directly with Detroit's Big Three, but it changed the focus from bigger to smaller and from gas guzzling to gas saving.

Avis adopted the same strategy by choosing not to compete with industry leader Hertz. Rather than promote themselves as the best in one aspect or another, they turned the tables and made a case for being number two and "trying harder." It worked because everyone loves the underdog. Avis jumped from number seven, their actual rank when the promotion started, to the number two car rental company in the industry.

PIONEERING SPIRIT

The Pleasant Co. succeeded in a market dominated by Barbies or Barbie wannabes by changing the appeal of its dolls. When they began, all the dolls on the market had pinup looks and dressed like they were going either to a mall or a ball. Pleasant Rowland, the founder of the company, shifted the focus to an educational one and used the dolls to teach American history, family values, and self-reliance.

Each of Rowland's dolls represented a different era in history. Samantha Parkington fought for women's suffrage, Addy Walker escaped from slavery, Kirsten Larsen built a life on the frontier. The dolls even had their own series of novels in which the heroines went on adventures and dealt with moral dilemmas. The Pleasant Co. decided not to compete for shelf space with Mattel's billion-dollar Barbie business, rather they sold their dolls through mail order. Though Pleasant's sales aren't threatening Mattel, their heroines are making hundreds of millions of dollars per year.

The Pleasant Co. has kept on with that pioneering spirit by creating the American Girl Place, a 35,000-square-foot retail outlet in downtown Chicago. This huge marketplace features, among other things, a tearoom, live entertainment, and elaborate displays detailing the life stories of the historical figures the company's dolls are modeled from. The American Girl Place has become a hot tourist attraction in its first year, having hosted more than 750,000 visitors.

DESIGN DOLLS

Taking the doll business even one step further, iDoll, a new Web site, is literally breaking old doll molds. Rather than buy an off-the-shelf Barbie or Ken, or one of the Pleasant Co.'s superheroines, iDoll's site lets girls use technology to design their own dolls from scratch. The Web site caters to preteen girls and allows them to choose different facial characteristics, clothes, and accessories in any of a huge number of possible combinations.

TEAMING UP

Another way the little guy can succeed is to team up with other little guys to form a big team. Mom-and-pop operations who combine with other mom-and-pops can become powerful national competitors. Many major corporations, like Waste Management, Service Corps of America, and Kinko's, were developed by combining companies. Recently 9,800 independent travel agencies joined to set up a Web site called Vacation.com and billed itself as the leading source of fun vacations on the Web.

DON'T COMPETE, CO-OPERATE

Alliances can offer small businesses all sorts of benefits, from lower prices to volume purchasing agreements and from education and training to national advertising.

Land O Lakes sells about $6 billion worth of dairy products and is one of the oldest cooperatives in the country. The company began operating over eighty years ago and is now made up of more than eleven thousand family-owned farms of all sizes and types from all over the continent. The company provides marketing, education, training, financing, purchasing, and extensive research for its independent farmer shareholders.

In 1985 two carpet retailers, Howard Brodsky and Alan Greenberg, recognized the need for little guys to band together in order to compete with big discounters like Home Depot. They formed Carpet One and today this co-op has more than 1,300 stores and earns $3 billion in sales annually. Lavone Pirner of Wichita had one store doing about $3 million in sales when he became a Carpet One member and stockholder. Taking advantage of Carpet One's advertising strength, ability to get better deals, exclusive arrangements with the big carpet and flooring manufacturers, and its educational and financing programs, Pirner's Carpet One Wichita now consists of ten stores that total $30 million in sales.

So don't compete, *co-op*erate.

DON'T BE A DAVID

OK, so David beat Goliath with a slingshot. But it's going to take more than a slingshot to beat the Goliaths in your marketplace. Truth is, you don't want to beat them. You don't even want to play on the same playing field. Going head-to-head with the big guys is a losing battle. In order to succeed, you've got to differentiate yourself from these companies. You must offer customers something they aren't getting and are unable to get from the megacorporations.

➠ **KEEP IN MIND**
➠ Create community, customize products and services.
➠ Act big.
➠ Be nimble.
➠ Grow your business by co-oping or by partnering.

[1] *New York Times*, 2 December 1999, p. C14.
[2] Ibid.
[3] *Inc. Magazine*, October 2000, p. 68.
[4] *Authors Guild Bulletin*, Fall 2000, p. 19.
[5] *Wall Street Journal*, 5 March 1999, p. B1.
[6] Ibid.
[7] *Fortune*, 18 December 2000, p. 292J.
[8] Ibid.
[9] Ibid.
[10] Ibid.
[11] *New York Times*, 22 September 1999, p. 34.
[12] Ibid.
[13] *New York Times*, 22 September 1999, p. B1.
[14] Ibid.
[15] Ibid.
[16] *New York Times*, 22 May 2000, p. C4.

CHAPTER 23

Risk Taking

RISK TAKING IS NATURAL

Innovation involves risk. To create something new and break from the pack, you have to be willing to take chances. In fact, the biggest risk in fast-changing times is not taking any risk at all.

Can you imagine if every baby learning to walk thought, "Hey, I might fall and hurt myself." If, as babies, we took the same approach to risk taking that many do now, we'd be a nation of crawlers.

Actually, we are born risk takers. How else would you have learned to walk, talk, ride a bike, or ski? You can't learn anything new without taking a risk and confronting challenges.

UH-OHS

Yet when I ask people in my programs to think of a word that describes risk, the response is usually *dangerous, foolish, crazy, scary, stupid,* and *failure.* Most people think of risk takers as bungee-jumping, rapids-riding, summit-scaling loonies who think nothing about taking their lives into their hands. Whether it's an adventurer risking life and limb or an entrepreneur risking house and savings, risk takers are viewed as wild and crazy.

Because of the negative connotations about risk and risk takers, it's no wonder that even though lip service is given to the importance of risk taking, the vast majority still gravitate toward tried-and-true conservative practices.

ACCENTUATING THE NEGATIVE

The result of this negative loading is that most people focus solely on the negative consequences of taking a risk. James T., an orthopedic surgeon, had been considering adding a partner to his practice, but he considered this a risky proposition for several reasons. He feared he'd have to spend a large sum of money to move to bigger offices or possibly invest in a new building. Likewise, he was also concerned that having a partner in the practice might decrease his income and that his patients might like the new doc better. He was afraid that he and his partner would disagree on certain business or professional issues. By focusing only on the negative consequences of the move, it was no wonder that James shied away from it.

BALANCING UPSIDE AND DOWNSIDE

When I asked James to list the potential rewards of taking this risk, he replied that taking on a partner might enable him to work less hours and spend more time with his family. He also thought there was a good possibility of making more money with two docs, which would allow them to modernize the office and get some of the latest equipment. There was also the possibility of developing a positive relationship that would enable both to learn and grow.

Thinking about only the negative consequences of a risk will prevent you from taking it. The key is to balance the upside benefits with the downside consequences so you can arrive at a realistic view of the action you are considering. After looking at both the downsides and upsides of the situation, James T. ended up moving ahead.

GETTING THE WHOLE PICTURE

Think about a risk you are considering and make two columns: the upside benefits and the downside consequences. Next to each entry estimate the possibility of that negative consequence or positive benefit actually happening. When James looked at entries like "My patients will like the new guy better," he broke out laughing and crossed it out. When he thought about partnering with someone he wouldn't get along with, he said that was a valid concern and "means that I will have to do more homework and check out anyone with whom I am thinking about getting involved."

Considering the potential negative consequences of taking a risk helps you to prepare for them. But remember to examine both sides of the equation. By analyzing the upside and the downside of a new challenge, you will have a much better sense of whether to move forward. Then if you decide to act, preparing for the possible negative consequences will have eliminated much of the recklessness of risk taking.

NOT WILD AND CRAZY GUYS

The truth is that most risk takers are neither wild nor crazy. The most successful risk takers are usually precise, sober people. *Time* magazine, in a feature on risk taking, said that "the most extreme risk taker talks like an astronaut about safety gear, of weather carefully calculated, of redundant strengths to cushion failure."[1]

We don't see all the preparation that precedes taking the risk. To negate the danger, stunt men and women take every imaginable precaution, carefully choreograph each stunt, and do a great deal of training and preparation. The men and women you see riding the rapids of wild rivers spend more time on land scouting the rapids and planning their route than they do in the water. Research done by pioneering sport psychologist Bruce Ogilvie, M.D., sheds further light on this subject. After studying extreme risk takers such as sky divers, Grand Prix drivers, and aerobatic pilots, Ogilvie came to the conclusion that risk takers "are extremely cautious people . . . that an extraordinary amount of intelligence goes into preparing for their activities. They have analyzed every factor that can operate against them."[2]

FROM MOUNTAINS TO BUSINESS

The most successful risk takers in business aren't those who jump blindly into some new venture. Prior to moving on to something new, they spend a great deal of time carefully doing their homework. Yvon Chouinard, the founder of the outdoor clothing company Patagonia, represents a prime example of this type of thinking. Because of his reputation as a world-class mountaineer and his incredible success as an outerwear clothing designer, many people consider Chouinard a daring risk taker. But the homework Chouinard did prior to having his successful line of baggie shorts produced in Panama— a big risk since the production standards were of unknown quality—gives a new insight into the man.

After careful inspection of the quality of the work, and in-depth discussions with the Panamanian management, Chouinard had his managers examine the machinery from top to bottom to see if it was adequate and well maintained. He then had his quality-control people train the Panamanian operators to ensure Patagonia's high standards and then stay on to oversee the process. The result was that Patagonia lowered costs and prices on the whole line.

LOOKING TOO FAR

Many individuals inadvertently sabotage themselves from taking risks by focusing solely on the goal. I saw this frequently on the ski slopes during the Inner Skiing seminars I conducted. When I took skiers to a challenging slope, the first thing they did was look all the way down to the bottom of the run. From this angle the run inevitably looked too hard, too long, and too steep and caused them to back off and want to head to the lodge for hot chocolate.

My advice was "See if there's one turn that you think you can make. If not, we will take an easier run." Most would see a turn they could take. I would then have them make it and stop to look for another one that they could make. This shift in their focus from the overall goal to the next step increased their confidence and got them safely down the mountain.

Concentrating on the end result, your goal provides direction and motivation. But to get yourself moving, whether it's on a ski slope or in business, it's important to make the first step, one that you are confident you can accomplish. Several positive can-do steps, as with the skiers, will get you to where you want to go sooner than you thought.

INCREMENTAL TO EXPONENTIAL

One of the keys for successful risk taking and bringing about an exponential change in your work or your life is taking incremental steps. But in adapting this strategy make sure that your first step is a win. Starting with a win, as with the skiing example, increases confidence, motivation, and more importantly, commitment to the process. After taking several small successful steps, the following ones become progressively faster and easier. Before you know it, you have arrived at your goal.

"Every change process that I've seen that was sustained, and that spread has started small,"[3] says management guru Peter Senge, author of the best-selling *The Fifth Discipline* and head of MIT's Center for Organizational Learning. "Usually these programs start with one team," continues Senge. At

Shell he says the critical generative work was done by a small top team that in a matter of a year spread to the top one hundred fifty managers, who "percolated ideas among themselves and . . . in turn formed new clusters of teams.

"In case after case," Senge continues, "the change effort begins small . . . Just as nothing in nature starts big, so the way to start creating change is with a pilot group—a growth seed."[4]

Pursuing Small Ideas

Donald Winkler, the innovative chairman and chief executive of Finance One Corporation, the consumer finance company owned by Bank One, is one of many leaders that has experienced how seemingly small change leads to big results. "The fervid search for the big idea distracts too many people from recognizing that organizations are transformed more deeply and continuously by the relentless pursuit of small ideas."[5] says Winkler. "Most of the time we compete on the basis of minute differentiations and small increments of value as perceived by the customers. That is precisely why a continual stream of small changes can, over time, have a far more powerful impact than many sweeping strategic decisions."[6]

Don't Bet the Farm

Another benefit of taking small steps is that . . . if they don't work, or something goes awry, or the marketplace changes as it continually does . . . you can learn, correct, and keep moving. Or chalk it off to experience.

If you bet the farm, you can easily land in the mud. As was mentioned in chapter two about the perils of rushing, dramatic changes often result in dramatic failure because time hadn't been taken to learn from experience and work out any bugs.

Don't Think Small

I am not telling you to think small. Big ideas, bold innovations, dramatic new solutions to old problems, are important for keeping ahead. But it's not the grandness of the idea that determines how successful you will be. It's how well you execute it. Success in anything lies in the implementation. And successful action most often begins with small steps.

Remember *think big but start small. Small wins lead to big victories.*

THE BIGGEST MISTAKE IS NOT MAKING ANY

Fear of failure is the major obstacle that prevents people from taking risks. But as most risk takers will tell you, you can't learn anything new without making mistakes. In fact, if you aren't making mistakes, you most likely aren't trying anything new or creative, which is an even bigger mistake.

The "total quality movement" had a saying, "Do it right the first time." I always thought that this discouraged risk taking and innovation. How can you do something right when you have never done it before? If people are afraid of making mistakes, they will always be conservative and play it too safe.

Companies that actively encourage innovation realize that failure and mistakes are a by-product. "If you try new things," says Jeffrey Skilling, the president of Enron Energy Services, one of the major players in the new deregulated utility industry, "some will work, some won't."[7]

"You're going to make mistakes. You can't sit there and punish people for trying," says Enron's chairman and CEO, Lou Pai. Pai himself is a good example of this philosophy. He was in charge of Enron's efforts to become the premier marketer of electric service to residential customers as states like California deregulated. This effort resulted in a two-year roller-coaster ride that cost big bucks and ultimately forced Enron to shelve the project.

A high-profile venture capitalist told me that one of the first questions he asks entrepreneurs seeking money is whether they have ever failed at anything. His reasoning is that anyone who has never come back from failure might not have what it takes to build a success. He didn't see failure as a weakness but as something that increases determination to succeed.

In a *New York Times* article entitled "If at First You Don't Succeed, Celebrate!" columnist Abby Ellin quoted Gretchen Rubin, the author of *Power, Money, Fame, Sex,* who wrote that "failure is the price of being on the bleeding edge, on the forefront of something. In the past you would have never wanted to be branded a failure, but now it shows you are creative, a risk taker. And that's what everybody praises."[8]

Justin Sewell, the chief executive of Despair Inc., which sells over a million dollars' worth of what he calls de-motivational products, such as "Failure!" T-shirts, says, "Young people especially are no longer ashamed of failing. It has been properly recognized as a natural and understandable consequence of taking risks. I think our culture admires a risk taker who fails more than a coward who never succeeds."[9]

My Bad

"Failure isn't a crime," said legendary Citibank chairman Walter Wriston, "failure to learn from failure is the crime." Many people, however, keep failing because they fail to take responsibility for their mistakes and thus never learn what really caused them. They blame other people, the situation, or the market for their misfortunes. It's the old finger-pointing exercise. When people blame each other, everyone gets defensive, and this creates an environment in which no learning takes place. Then, to avoid the finger being pointed at them ever again, people start playing it too safe.

Basketball players have a little ritual that we can all use. When a player makes a bad pass or misses a defensive assignment, he yells out, "My bad." Admitting that he erred defuses the situation, and then his teammates usually don't hold on to the need to blame. Also, by owning up to a mistake, you acknowledge what you did to cause it, which usually prevents you from repeating it. "Awareness itself is curative," said Fritz Perls, M.D., the founder of gestalt therapy. Trying to avoid responsibility for an error, on the other hand, prevents learning from taking place, which then often leads to a repeat.

Katie Paine, a former director of corporate communications for Lotus and the founder and CEO of the Delahaye Group, gets people to admit mistakes by having a "mistake of the month" contest. "Several years ago I overslept and missed a flight to a big client meeting," she said. "I then walked into my next staff meeting, told the story, plunked $50 down on the table, and said, 'If you can top my mistake, that money is yours.'" People quickly started owning up to mistakes, and suddenly they had a flood of them. One of their sales guys had gone on a sales call without business cards; two of their people arrived at a Coca-Cola meeting without their presentation materials.

"At every staff meeting, we write up the mistakes of the month on a whiteboard," says Paine. "Since 1989 we've recorded two thousand mistakes. And once the mistake hits the whiteboard, it tends to never be repeated. This practice has had a real impact on our work."[10]

Fabulous Flops

To puncture the fear of failing on a new project, many companies celebrate fabulous flops. Remember Zap Mail from Federal Express? No? It was a huge failure that cost FedEx about $300 million. You'd think that FedEx would be ashamed of this fabulous flop. But the opposite is true. People at FedEx are proud of Zap Mail because it shows their willingness to take risks, to change and try new ideas.[11]

Admitting mistakes is the first step to learning from them, which is pretty good insurance that you won't repeat them. You'll score a lot more points by admitting, "My bad." Is there someone or some team right now that you could admit that to?

RISKING IS NATURAL

Avoiding risks prevents us from growing, learning, innovating, and performing at peak levels. Worse, it prevents us from experiencing the joy and excitement of exploring the unknown and coming up with new ideas, opportunities, and possibilities.

⫸ KEEP IN MIND

- ⫸ Risk taking is natural.
- ⫸ Risk takers are not wild and crazy.
- ⫸ Small steps lead to big victories.
- ⫸ The biggest mistake is not making any.
- ⫸ It's OK to say, "My bad."

[1] *Time*, 29 August 1983, p. 56.
[2] *Esquire*, September 1985, p. 42.
[3] *Fast Company*, May 1999, p. 186.
[4] Ibid.
[5] *New York Times*, 14 June 1998.
[6] Ibid.
[7] *New York Times*, 27 June 1999, p. B13.
[8] *New York Times*, 20 August 2000, p. B10.
[9] Ibid.
[10] *Fast Company*, November 1998, p. 58.
[11] *Fast Company*, October 1999, p. 342.

CHAPTER 24

Stoke Fires, Don't Soak Them

FIREHOSING

You're off to a meeting and you're stoked. You've got this great idea for a new service that is a real barn burner, and you can't wait to tell your team. Well, hold on to your shirt. The most common response to new ideas isn't fire, passion, and excitement—it's the firehose.

"Firehosing" is the voice of resistance that always tells you why your ideas won't work, can't be done, and probably aren't in the budget. As Albert Einstein once said, "The greatest ideas are often met with violent opposition from mediocre minds." The philosopher Schopenhauer said, "All truths are initially either ridiculed or violently opposed."[1]

Firehosing is often tied into past experience, so it keeps you in the comfort zone. The most active firehoser is often the wise old veteran who has "seen it all," and his words seem to inject some control into an unpredictable world. It is the safe response. But playing it safe is dangerous when you are in a changing environment. Staying in the comfort zone will become very uncomfortable in an environment that is constantly in flux.

Though a firehose may sound reasonable, it is destructive in three ways. First, it kills an idea that may be good but needs a little tweaking. The firehose, however, will ensure that the idea is slaughtered. Second, it kills the spirit. Firehosing puts out people's fire, douses their spark, and damp-

Dilbert © UFS. Reprinted by permission.

ens their enthusiasm. Third, firehosing kills the motivation to come up with new ideas in the future. Once a person gets firehosed, odds are they'll be too afraid to offer up a new idea ever again.

And guess who we firehose most often—ourselves. Before we even write down an idea and give someone else a chance to respond to it, that voice inside our head comes up with a multitude of reasons why it won't work and can't be done.

OLD HABITS DIE HARD

One of the reasons that the firehose is so common is that we're all creatures of habit. It is these same habits and traditional modes of thinking that stifle growth and creativity and almost ensure that competitors will pass you by. Relying on old habits also puts you to sleep mentally and deadens your spirit.

Try this little habit-breaking exercise and you'll understand what I mean:

Cross your arms. Now cross them again with the other arm on top. Notice how it feels. Weird, right? Like you've lost your armpit.

Clap your hands. Now clap them with what was your bottom hand on top. How does that feel? Strange and uncomfortable, right?

Your response to these two habit-breaking exercises is one reason that people firehose innovative new ideas. Breaking a habit, whether it's mental or physical, feels awkward. The new way hasn't been tried before, so it's untested and there is uncertainty about whether it will work. The most common and easiest response, therefore, is for people to resist change and continue old practices.

Getting the Habit of Breaking Old Habits

One way to keep from firehosing yourself is to make it a habit to break one habit every week. Do something different both at work and at home. Start with something easy. Take a different route home. Eat with your opposite hand. Put your pants on starting with your opposite leg. Brush your teeth with your other hand. Go someplace for lunch you haven't gone before and eat something you've never tried.

At work you might try to attack the mountain of paper by starting at the bottom, or start at the end of your e-mail list rather than the beginning.

I give over seventy-five speeches a year, and none of them are the same. I always try something different: a new story, example, or exercise. Approaching my work with a habit-breaking mentality keeps me fresh and on a creative edge. It also gets me excited and a little anxious about whether the new material will work. And even if it doesn't, I learn something from trying it.

DODGING THE FEAR SPRAY

Fear is a major cause of firehosing. People are scared that a new idea won't work or that they won't be able to keep up. The response therefore is to hose the idea so they can be safe and comfortable.

In order to dodge the fear-driven firehose, it helps to understand that most fears are exaggerated, and the imagined consequences are usually blown out of proportion. To scared skiers the slopes look twice as steep and long, and a broken leg will surely result. Similarly the new sales goal always looks impossibly high in January.

Reality Checks/Worst-Case Scenario

Since most fears are exaggerated and irrational, a strong dose of reality will often enable potential hosers to see what is *really* true about a situation and offer perspective about their ability to deal with it as well the real possible consequences of failing. One way to do a reality check is to ask:

1. What is the worst thing that can happen if this idea doesn't work?

2. On a scale of 1 to 10, what is the likelihood of that thing happening?

A reality check will usually show you that a given situation is not as scary as you think, and that your ability to handle the consequences is far better than your fears would lead you to believe.

Due to the rapid growth in his area, especially in the industrial sector, a successful builder of residential homes saw a great opportunity to broaden his base of operations but told me, "Whenever I think of expanding into the commercial arena, I panic. It would mean leasing new types of equipment, hiring more-experienced crews, working with higher-level engineers, making new contacts. There's no guarantee all that would even work. And the thought of possibly failing, when I'm doing fine right now, seems so scary that I don't want to think about it."

"What's the worst thing that could happen?" I asked.

"I'm afraid of making some terrible blunder and going belly-up," he said. "And if that happened, I'd lose everything—my trucks, my equipment, maybe even my house, not to mention the reputation I've been building for twenty years. Maybe I ought to forget the whole thing."

I intervened with the next step in the reality check, asking, "On a scale of 1 to 10—if 10 equals certainty—what are the chances of all of that happening?"

He stopped for a minute, stared at the ceiling, and then said, "Hmmm, I've never looked at it that way before. It's probably only a 4 or at most a 5." His whole body seemed to relax as he mentioned these numbers. "That's not nearly as bad as I thought." He then laughed, saying, "Heck, a minute ago I had myself headed off to debtors' prison. But a 4 or a 5 is a risk I am willing to take. Heck, even if the worst did happen, I can always get a job in the building trades."

I have used this worst-case-scenario reality check with all types of people in all types of situations, and the results are always similar. People realize the chances of that imagined disaster occurring are less than they first thought. This enables them to relax and more accurately size up the situation.

Another type of reality check is to ask yourself if you have ever been in a similar situation. Most often you have. And you have probably handled it far better than your fear-driven mind remembers. Keeping a victory log (see chapter 25) of your past successes and reviewing it when starting something new is very helpful for increasing confidence and reducing firehosing.

Reality checks and victory logs will enable you to more realistically assess your ability to handle a situation. Potential "hosers" will realize that the worst that is likely to happen is never as bad as they imagined. As a famous coach once quipped, "If all things that we thought were life-and-death actually turned out to be, there'd be a lot more dead people around."

WIIFM AND TOP-DOWN HOSES

Another trigger for the firehose is the "What's in it for me?" response. Motivation slackens when there is no perceived personal gain. If there's no incentive for trying a new approach, out comes the hose.

The firehose will also often emerge when a new idea is handed down from the top. When people aren't asked for their input, they feel dumped on and resent it: "How come no one asked for my input?" they wonder. When someone doesn't feel part of the solution, they often will become part of the problem. On the other hand, when people feel involved in a change or new idea, they are much more likely to be positive about it. Ownership is a great motivator.

When you are introducing a new idea, the best way to plug up the firehose is to anticipate resistance. Make sure to mention what's in it for the group. Get them involved in some phase of the implementation. At a major utility where a new accounting system was being introduced, management countered defused resistance by having each department customize the system for their own use.

NERFING THE HOSE

One way to dodge the spray of the firehose is to use this fun and effective technique. At a brainstorming session with the leaders of a large hospital chain that I was facilitating, I placed a large red Nerf ball on the table, explained about firehosing, and announced that anyone firehosing any idea was fair game to have the ball thrown at them.

After about fifteen minutes, one vice president responded to a suggestion with, "That's too expensive and we've already got our budget worked out. Furthermore, the docs and nurses will never go along with it." And boom! Someone hit him with the Nerf ball. Everyone laughed—even the hoser. And that was the signal for open fire on all hosing. It was incredible. Every time someone came out with a firehose, they got Nerfed.

What was even more incredible was that everyone's behavior changed. They started piggybacking on other people's ideas and coming up with a lot of out-of-the-box suggestions. The tone of the meeting became lighter, more fun, and less inhibited. Furthermore, when you are having fun, you operate out of the same side of your brain that sparks creativity. Always remember, fun is a precursor to creativity.

At one point the president of the group took the ball and actually threw it in his own face, announcing, "If you would have heard what I was thinking, you would have Nerfed me too, so I beat you to it!"

The result of the meeting was the development of a line of information software for external health facilities that generated revenues of over $75 million in three years. And it wouldn't have happened without that crazy red Nerf ball.

Almost weekly I receive Nerf balls, or alternatives such as water pistols and plant sprayers, with company logos and notes telling me, "We use these at all of our meetings." In fact, several months ago a client mailed me a supersoaker with a note that said, "We've got big hosers in our place."

The key to keeping out in front of change and developing innovative new ideas and opportunities is to *stoke* fires, not *soak* them. The next time you go to a meeting, bring along a Nerf ball or squirt gun and be ready for some action, fun, and creativity. In fact, keep one handy in your office. I have a water pistol in my desk drawer, and every time I catch myself firehosing one of my own ideas, I give myself a little squirt.

DODGING THE SPRAY

These statements are a sure sign that the firehose is attached to the hydrant and will soon start spraying gallons of water:

- **"That isn't the way we do things around here."**
- **"We've never done anything like that before."**
- **"This is the way we've always done it."**

Resisting change and doing things the way you always have ensures you'll be bypassed by competitors and perhaps soon be out of business. Using yesterday's strategies and practices in today's game will almost guarantee you won't be around tomorrow. As one executive said, "The tried and true gets you dead and buried."

"Great idea, but . . ."
This is code for "I think the idea stinks." Anything that comes before the "but" is bull.

"Don't stick your neck out."
Burying your head in the sand like an ostrich is a strategy that can't possibly work in a competitive environment. These days if you don't stick your neck out, you'll lose your head. Playing it safe is dangerous. The comfort zone is a misnomer. The only thing that is comfortable in this type of environment is the excitement that results from change and innovation.

"It's just a fad."
Yes, and so was the cell phone, the microwave oven, the fax machine. Today's fad is often tomorrow's basic necessity.

"It's too . . ."
hard; complicated; expensive; quick; slow; showy; time-consuming. Anytime you give in to the word "too," it is too late.

"It'll never work; can't be done."
And neither could most of the things you are doing right now. What seems impossible today won't be by tomorrow. Anything is possible.

"They have no experience in our industry."
And neither did many of the very successful heads of major companies. Beginners bring new perspectives to old games.

"It is unrealistic or impractical."
Don't forget that what was reality yesterday is probably outdated today and will be obsolete tomorrow. And what was

unrealistic yesterday is probably doable today and will be common practice tomorrow.

If it ain't broke, don't fix it."

If you wait until it's broke before you try to fix it, you'll end up with nothing left to fix and something that is probably broke.

"Don't rock the boat."

Huge waves of change are already rocking the boat and will sink it if you're not prepared to change course.

"It's not in the budget."

Of course not. This year's budget was made up last year, when circumstances were entirely different.

"Let's wait and see."

A delay tactic based on the hope that down the road the whole idea will be forgotten. But by the time you wait to see if something works, the opportunity will have flown away, on someone else's wings.

))))➡ KEEP IN MIND

- ➡ Get in the habit of breaking habits.
- ➡ Anticipate resistance.
- ➡ Reality checks and victory logs help to conquer fear.
- ➡ Bring a Nerf ball or water pistol to meetings.
- ➡ Stoke people's fires, don't soak them.

---

[1] Joey Reiman, *Thinking for a Living* (Marietta, Ga.: Longstreet, 1998), p. 30.

Keep a \

sult, you don't pe
cycle continue
past event.

T hough most of us have experienced both victories and de-
feats, we tend to take our victories and breakthroughs for
granted and remember the breakdowns much more
vividly. You putt beautifully on seven greens, pretty good on a
few others, and blow a three-footer. Which do you think
about later? The one you blew. I've seen skiers who, after a fall
at the beginning of a run, ski the rest beautifully. Yet at the
bottom they are swearing at themselves for having a bad run.
You leave a meeting in which you handled three questions
with flair, one fair, and one not so well. Which are you thinking about? If you're human, it will be the one you fumbled.

THE 10/90 SYNDROME

Focusing on the negative exaggerates the mistake and results
in what I call the 10/90 response. The 10 percent of your performance that is poor puts a stranglehold on the other 90 percent in your memory. This unbalance convinces you that you
had an awful experience. Your confidence plummets, which
in turn affects your mood as well as everything you do and
everyone you relate to—including your spouse and kids when
you get home.

Then when a similar situation arises, the experience that
is most vivid in your mind is the last one you "blew." As a re-

...rform up to your skill level. This vicious
..., all because of an inaccurate evaluation of a

PAST VICTORIES

If dwelling on past failures saps your confidence and zaps your motivation, focusing on past successes achieves the opposite. Success is a great motivator and confidence builder. You confront a difficult challenge and succeed, so you immediately feel great and are motivated and excited.

To help increase confidence and motivation, as well as your performance and productivity, you can train yourself, your people, and even your kids to focus on past victories rather than failures.

A vivid example of this type of thinking took place in the 1989 Super Bowl, in which the San Francisco 49ers were playing the Cincinnati Bengals. With less than two minutes left, the Niners were five points down and had to go ninety yards for a touchdown. Looking at his players in the huddle, quarterback Joe Montana, one of sport's greatest pressure performers, said, "Hey, this is just like 1982."

What was he doing? Montana was reminding his teammates of a similar situation back in 1982, when the Niners were playing the Dallas Cowboys for the NFC championship. Back then, with two minutes remaining, Montana led the team the length of the field and in the final seconds threw a game- and championship-winning touchdown pass.

By reflecting on that past experience, Montana got his teammates to realize that not only had they previously been in a similar situation but they had been successful. Remembering that past victory over the Bengals calmed the players and boosted their confidence. The result was that they went down the field, and in the waning seconds, Montana threw the touchdown pass that defeated the Cincinnati Bengals and won the Super Bowl for San Francisco.

Looking Back

When I taught skiing, I would watch skiers, halfway down a difficult run, stop and look down the rest of the slope with dread. I'd encourage them instead to look back up the hill at what they had *already* skied. The change in attitude was instantaneous. Looking at what they had already accomplished increased their confidence and excitement about skiing the rest of the run.

There is nothing like winning to create a winning attitude. The more you remind yourself or others of past victories, the more you will build a positive reality base for handling challenging situations.

When David Cone, a brilliant pitcher for the New York Yankees, was unraveling, in 2000, on his way to posting a 4–14 won-loss record and an equally bad earned-run average, he was so frustrated that he hurled a hand-painted ashtray across manager Joe Torre's office, smashing a prized photo of Joe DiMaggio and Mickey Mantle. Yet Torre continued to pitch him.

When players get down on themselves like this, Torre, one of baseball's great managers and motivators, who has led the Yankees to four World Series championships, always says to them, "I remember what you did for me and for this organization. Why don't *you* remember?"

Not Positive Thinking

Focusing on past victories is not positive thinking. Trying to think positively when you are quaking in your boots is like putting on a clean shirt when you really need a shower. Nor is it wishful thinking, just hoping that you will do well.

Reflecting on past victories is reality-based thinking. The

successes you have had are real. They did happen. It's no longer "maybe you can"—you already have.

Reality thinking involves accurately evaluating your efforts. Count the good shots as well as the bad, the great responses as well as the flubs. Balancing the losses with the wins provides you with a genuine view of your efforts. If you are like most people, you probably aren't giving yourself credit for being as good as you are.

VICTORY LOGS AND HIGHLIGHT FILMS

To increase confidence and motivation for any situation, ranging from sports to work to school, we have created victory logs and personal highlight films, in which people record their past wins.

"I used to panic before my monthly presentations to the board," the president of a major software company told me. After a coaching consult, he decided to keep a victory log. Following each meeting he would jot down reminders about the wins he had in that meeting. "Now prior to every presentation, I thumb through my victory log, which helps to calm me down and feel more confident and ready."

Nordstrom's, one of the most successful department store chains, noted for their spectacular customer service, has the motto "Respond to unreasonable customer requests." This credo has resulted in salespeople doing the out-of-the-ordinary, such as hand-delivering items to the airport for a customer's last-minute business trip, changing a customer's flat tire, or paying their parking ticket. Nordstrom's encourages these acts by keeping scrapbooks of "heroic" acts.

Personally I find keeping a victory log so valuable that I use it before every speech I give. Flipping through the pages energizes me and bolsters my confidence.

On the Wall

Susan Harris, a telemarketer for San Diego's well-known La Jolla Playhouse, came up with a unique form of victory log. "Every time I make a sale, I draw a heart in color on the card, write the date and amount of the sale on the heart, and tack in onto my wall. Then whenever I feel myself going into a slump or losing energy, I take a break and look at my victory wall. Focusing on my successes," she told me, "reminds me that I know what I am doing, doing it well, and that the product is exceptional. The result is that my brief victory-wall break reenergizes and inspires me, and my confidence and enthusiasm return.

"Looking at all those victories has never failed to bring me out of a slump," says Harris, who since starting her victory wall has become the number one salesperson in the organization. Her problem now is that "I am running out of space on the wall. I guess they'll have to give me a bigger office."

Improving Your Life

Victory logs can help improve the quality of your life as well as your performance. When John Ernst headed a major advertising agency, he ran through a daily review before going to bed. Most of the review, he said, consisted of what didn't go right and what he'd have to fix the next day. "As a result, I'd feel frustrated, anxious, depressed, and I wasn't sleeping.

"Keeping a victory log, first of all, helped me to realize that things were going much better than I thought. But more than that, this simple little exercise changed everything in my work and my life. I'm much more positive, upbeat, and easier to be around now. And I like myself better."

Starting Your Victory Log

Entries into your victory log don't have to be long or detailed. All it takes is a line or even a word or two that evokes a memory of a positive event. I have found the simple act of noting these positive experiences, putting them down on paper, makes them more real and imprints them deeply in the psyche.

Keeping a victory log will enable you to build a positive reality base for successfully handling tough situations. Reading your victory log before pressure situations will increase your confidence, turn your anxiety into excitement, and enable you to perform at peak levels more often.

⟫➠ KEEP IN MIND

➠ Throughout your life you will have numerous successes. You will accomplish goals, have moments of great clarity and vision, and some of your dreams will come true. Your victory log is a special place to record these personal victories.

➠ Read your victory log. It will remind you of your accomplishments and help you remember how terrific you really are.

➠ Your victory log will give you insights into your strengths and get you back on track when you are in a slump or running on empty.

➠ Read your victory log before making a big presentation, embarking on a major project, or prior to any pressure situation. You will find it a source of confidence, inspiration, and power.

➠ Reminding yourself of your past victories helps you identify with your potential rather than your problems. Your victory log reminds you to act from strength rather than weakness, and enables you to feel more powerful, confident, and in control of yourself in any situation.

➠ Each limit exceeded, each boundary crossed, verifies that most limits are self-imposed, that your potential and possibilities are far greater than you have imagined, and that you are capable of far more than you thought.

➡ The internal rewards of victory are joy, vitality, well-being, and the knowledge that throughout your life you will continue to exceed your own limits and break your own records.

[1] *Fortune*, 30 April 2001, p. 69.

CHAPTER 26

Fueling Your Fire

Leaders and peak performers in all fields often aren't the smartest or most skilled, but they are the ones with the most fire in their belly. They are passionate about what they do. Passion is a burning commitment that involves your whole being—body, mind, and spirit. It makes you feel more vital and alive and enables you to tap into inner strengths, resources, skills, and energy that you didn't even know existed.

Passion is the essential ingredient that will facilitate the implementation of the ideas and strategies discussed in this book. It is the key to turning ideas into action, to getting the creative juices flowing, and to performing at your peak in any area of your life. It's that inner fire that gets ordinary people to accomplish extraordinary things without feeling they are working so damn hard.

Perseverance is often touted as the key to success. But passion is the fuel that powers perseverance. Without that inner fire, perseverance soon fizzles.

YOU SEE WHAT YOU FEEL

Passion shapes your perception. The more fired up you are, the less difficult a task appears. Anything seems possible when you are stoked about it. Nothing seems too much trouble or too difficult. When you are passionate about what you are doing, obstacles that would normally seem insurmountable are seen as challenges to be overcome.

On the other hand, when the fire is low, it's like having no fuel in your tank. Everything appears overwhelming. The smallest obstacle seems mountainous. Everything becomes too much trouble, too difficult. When energy and enthusiasm are low, it feels as if you have to push through a wall of resistance to accomplish anything.

IT'S NOT WORK

When you are excited about what you are doing, you will willingly spend more time learning about it in order to improve. People who love golf, for instance, spend hours practicing at driving ranges, they buy books and magazines, watch tapes, keep up with the latest innovations, share tips, take lessons. All this extra effort is fueled by their passion for the game.

The same is true with anything you are excited about. When I worked in advertising, I spent many an evening watching television, but not the programs, the commercials. I was so fired up about my job that I would sit there alone trying to think of better ways to advertise the products. It wasn't work. It was fun.

PASSION LEADS TO INNOVATION

When you're passionate about something, you also become more resourceful. The result is that you will often discover and develop innovative new ideas, products, or services.

As a young man, Jack O'Neil loved the water. He surfed, scuba dived, fished, and always managed to work in or around the water. The problem that O'Neil and his friends encountered was that the water in the San Francisco Bay Area was cold. The wet suits that the surfers were then using leaked and didn't keep out the cold, so the time they could spend in the water was limited. Driven by his desire to spend more time in the water, O'Neil began searching for materials that would be leak-proof and provide warmth. He experimented with a variety of materials and designs.

The rest, they say, is history. O'Neil invented the wet suit as we know it today. Today it's rare to go to a beach without seeing O'Neil wet suits, surfboards, and other water sports products. And it all started with a young man's love of the water.

THE PASSION INDEX

At change management seminars that I conducted for Hewlett Packard, managers were instructed to bring in a change project—a new idea for a process, program, system, or strategy they wanted to implement back at work.

The first step was to rate their change project on a passion scale of 1 to 10, with 10 representing being fired up about the project and 1 equal to a dying ember. After five years of doing these seminars with managers from all over the world, we found that a project rated 7 or lower on the passion scale wouldn't get done. In these cases, we'd advise returning to the drawing board and redesigning the project so that they would be more excited about it. Or to rethink the project altogether using passion as their guiding element.

How passionate are you about what you are doing? What is your passion index about your job or the project you are working on? If it's below an 8, it's time to go back to the drawing board and rethink or reinvent what you are doing. Use passion as a guide.

LIGHT THE FIRE

Ultimately, passion will enable you to do more than you ever thought possible and to be more than you ever thought you could be. When you are passionate about what you are doing, you'll tap into skills and inner resources you didn't know existed. That inner fire is the key to transforming the innate potential that exists in all of us into peak performance.

When you are excited about what you are doing, you'll find that nothing is too hard, no peak too high, no dream impossible, and you'll enjoy the climb as much as reaching the summit.

➡ KEEP IN MIND

- ➡ Passion is high-octane fuel for the human engine.
- ➡ Do something to stoke your fire every day.
- ➡ Use a passion index on your job and projects.
- ➡ Chase your dreams.

CHAPTER 27

Leading an Innovative Life

Conventional thinking tells us that we must respond quickly to change. But winners in an increasingly challenging environment must be creators, not responders. They must invent the future. They must be innovators with the vision, courage, and daring to think beyond the boundaries of the known. But breakthrough thinking is not limited to the world of work. Rather, it is a style that enables anyone to excel in any area and lead a richer, more rewarding life.

FROM SPORTS TO RELATIONSHIPS

Innovative thinking can be learned and practiced in everything you do, from sports to cooking, from the arts to relationships. Athletics, the most visible high-pressure arena, has a great influence on many of our strategies and thinking. Its jargon is used as a metaphor in business: "I struck out," "Don't drop the ball," and "I hit a home run on that presentation."

Breakthroughs in sports have come from innovators like Jean-Claude Killy, Bill Walsh, Sonja Henie, Martina Navratilova, Dick Fosbury, and John Wooden. Bill Walsh, who won three Super Bowls as coach of the San Francisco 49ers, flipped the traditional thinking about offensive football on its head. Sonja Henie won the gold medal in figure skating in the 1928 Olympics by going out of the traditional skating "box" and introducing ballet into her routine. Chris Evert and Jimmy Connors, among others, challenged tradition in tennis by using a two-handed backhand.

Innovative thinkers like these, who keep pushing the envelope, provide us with great examples for expanding our vistas about what is physically and mentally possible.

BREAKING OUT OF THE BOX IN RELATIONSHIPS

Many of the innovative strategies discussed throughout this book will enable you to spend more quality time with your family. But when we spend time with loved ones, we often fall into old familiar habits and patterns. We go to the same places, see the same people, eat at the same restaurants, talk about the same subjects, and go on the same vacations. The result is that our relationships have become predictable, safe, comfortable, and dull. We lose the spark.

My wife, Marilyn, and I use several strategies mentioned in this book to recapture and reinvent the excitement. Recognizing that niches can turn into ruts, we rarely repeat the same vacation. We have hiked the Cotswolds, barged in Burgundy, sea kayaked in Baja, camped in Denali National Park in Alaska, and mountain biked in Canyonlands National Park in Utah. We are always looking for new experiences that will refresh and reinvigorate our lives and our relationship.

Once a month we "surprise the customer." One of us takes responsibility for planning a date that is out of our usual pattern, and doesn't reveal any of the plans to the other. The result on both sides has been eager anticipation and delight.

These surprise dates have almost always been fabulous. Marilyn once took me on a full moon kayak trip on the San Francisco Bay from Sausalito to Tiburon for dinner. Unbelievably romantic! We've also had some faux pas, but even those, because they were out of the ordinary, were fun and refreshing.

There is one hard-and-fast rule in this game. While on this date, we don't talk about the usual maintenance and logistic issues of our lives such as kids, school, work, schedules, and bills.

IGNITING THE SPARK

Thinking out of the box rekindles a spark, touching something that in many of us has been submerged for too long. We all have dreams tucked away. We all want to feel passionate about what we are doing and how we are living our lives. We all want to break free and live life to the fullest.

No one wants to look in the mirror late in life and feel they didn't give it their best shot. We don't want to give in to our fears. Being an innovative thinker means "going for it" and living life as an exciting adventure with passion, boldness, courage, and daring.

As you close this book, open your victory log and reexperience your creativity, passion, and boldness that exist in those breakthrough times. Remind yourself that those qualities are always there, waiting to be expressed in whatever you are doing, wherever you go.

Living your life as a breakthrough thinker will enable you to continually surprise yourself. You'll end up doing more than you ever thought you could, being more than you ever thought you were, and living a life that is more rewarding, more fulfilling, and a hell of a lot more fun. And, one in which you won't have to work so damn hard.

ABOUT THE AUTHOR

ROBERT J. KRIEGEL, Ph.D., is a pioneer in the field of human performance and the psychology of change. A former coach of both Olympic and professional athletes, Kriegel is the co-author of two of the most influential business books of the last decade, *Sacred Cows Make the Best Burgers* and *If It Ain't Broke . . . Break It!*—both national bestsellers. A commentator for NPR's Marketplace, he has served as a member of California's Governor's Council, taught in Stanford University's Executive Management Program, and has recently done two PBS specials.

Robert J. Kriegel, Ph.D.
Kriegel 2, Inc.
16344 Sharon Way
Grass Valley, CA 95949
PHONE (503) 272-1100
FAX (503) 272-7520
www.kriegel.com

SACRED COWS MAKE THE BEST BURGERS
Developing *Change-Ready* People and Organizations
The *BusinessWeek* Bestseller
by Robert Kriegel and David Brandt

Change is happening at breakneck speed: the competition is tougher, the customer is more sophisticated, margins are shrinking, entire industries are disappearing, and everybody is downsizing—trying to do more with less. Leading authorities in the field of change and human performance, Drs. Kriegel and Brandt show you how to keep ahead of these light-speed changes, not just keep up. You'll learn how to round up outdated practices that cost you time and money and gain the competitive edge by changing the game.

"A must-read!"
—Ken Blanchard, coauthor of *The One-Minute Manager*®

IF IT AIN'T BROKE...BREAK IT!
And Other Unconventional Wisdom
for a Changing Business World
Robert J. Kriegel and Louis Patler

Traditional business wisdom says to "work harder and faster," "stay the course," and "don't mess with success." Yet in today's rapidly changing times, these outmoded ideas can actually lead you to obsolescence and failure. In this unique book, you will learn how to unlock the creative thinker in yourself and explore different paths. You will discover how to break the rules of business—and break away from the pack. With hundreds of examples of Break-It Thinking, this book will help you apply new and profitable ideas to your own business.

"It's more than entertaining reading. It's survival skills
in these times of breakneck change."
—John A. Young, former president & CEO, Hewlett-Packard Company